Once

for
Anna-Mae & Isabelle

Once

Andrew McNeillie

seren

Seren is the book imprint of
Poetry Wales Press Ltd
Nolton Street, Bridgend, Wales
www.seren-books.com

© Andrew McNeillie, 2009

The right of Andrew McNeillie to be identified as the Author
of this Work has been asserted in accordance with the Copyright,
Designs and Patents Act, 1988.

ISBN 978-1-85411-496-9

A CIP record for this title is available from
the British Library

The publisher works with the financial assistance
of the Welsh Books Council

Printed by The Cromwell Press Group, Trowbridge

Contents

He that observeth the wind shall not sow; and he that regardeth the clouds shall not reap.

ECCLESIASTES

Tu te rappellera la beauté des caresses...

CHARLES BAUDELAIRE

THE KNOWN WORLD

The plane came out at the mouth of the Dee before turning west for Ireland. As soon as I saw the black river, at its dissolution in the Irish Sea, on such a clear winter's day, I had mentally to blink twice to be sure I could trust my eyes. No, it was not for a minute the murky Mersey, it was the dark-hearted Dee, the black Welsh river far dearer to my heart.

As to my heart, I could only find further warm pleasure in the fact that I flew aboard a plane of the AER ARANN line, my destination Galway. 'Arann' here refers to the 'Aran' Islands, at the mouth of Galway Bay, where, on Inis Mór, I lived for all but a year in my young manhood, a story to which this is the belated prequel.

The thought made me remember how in my youth I had loved to dream over the map of Britain and Ireland. I relished coastlines and rivers most, estuaries, islands, peninsulas, capes, headlands, bays and inlets. I loved them in outline and I loved the words for them. What is called the littoral, life at the margins, and its lexicon, enchanted me, seduced me. The sight of a harbour with fishing boats and the glimpsed lives of those aboard them chastened me especially. Perhaps I should have gone to sea. Whatever I am, I'm sure I should not have become what I am. Not at least without the great good fortune of having been born and brought up beside the Irish Sea in post-war North

Wales, with a writer for a father.

As I flew I remembered a similar flight to Ireland made when I was four. An unusual event in our lives, it was afforded by a book by my father called *No Resting Place*, subsequently filmed in Co. Wicklow, by Paul Rotha, with Abbey and Gate Theatre players. The mental footage of that journey reeled in my mind now. Here I was in its slipstream, physically, ghosting my childish progress in both body and mind. My former embodiment had flown aboard a Dakota, from Speke to Dublin. That was on another bright day in 1951, late July, like this one in February 2006, free of muffling cotton-wool cloud.

There's nothing like an aerial view for showing how fleeting life is, local and lost. The earth literally slips away before our eyes, after our eyes, into our wake. The earth abides forever says the text. But what remembrance of former things is there between generations? Houses rise and fall. Roads come and go. Families die out. Land is consumed by settlement. Villages grow into towns. Rivers are diverted or dammed. Valleys and worlds are drowned. (COFIWCH DRYWERYN reads the famous slogan by the road, the most famous slogan in Wales: Remember Tryweryn, the drowned village.) What do our individual labours and endeavours amount to, and our great passions, sorrows, loves and fears, our brave adventures, our little obscure lives, our moments of courage? Don't even mention our pettinesses and vices. Even if we seize the day? And who in reality seizes the day but the day seizes first?

What I write here now, if it sees the light of day, being too soon starved of readers will perish on the air like the May-fly under the alder, where the Dee runs dark as the Styx, beneath brooding Welsh clouds. Yet the printed word once hatched has power of survival second only to the stones. I put my faith in it, against all prospect of disaster. I put my faith in the word. The word made gooseflesh, tingling with remembrance, joy and sorrow, the soul made flesh, grounded in the world. We must make a virtue of what we do when it is plainly not a vice. What else? When we can do no other?

The printed words you're about to read are a relief map of my mind, of the known world, as I knew it once and as I see its lineaments now. I call the sum of them my ideal legendary story. Don't look here for date and fact and mere sequence of events. This is no curriculum vitae. Nor is it anything approaching such a godforsaken thing, such a travesty of being. (As the poet Les Murray revising the *Book of Common Prayer* has put it: 'In the midst of life, we are in employment'. As I would have added in my youth, in the midst of life we are in education.)

The view from the plane reminded me of co-ordinates that mesmerised me in my boyhood and youth beyond reason: triangulations, between the Red Wood, the Black Lake, the Wooded Hill, and places farther afield. Travel directly west on the same line of latitude as the Wooded Hill, with just a little latitude, and you'll come to Inis Mór: another limestone territory too. Go no less directly north across the Irish Sea and you'll reach the Ancient Kingdom of Galloway – Little Ireland – whence McNeillies derive.

How I loved to dream awake along those rectilinear lines. They were lines in a poem. They were my heart's armature. They defined and structured my legendary and imaginative territory. They entranced me and filled me with longing to adventure, to leave, to go the longest way round to come the shortest way home. Now I recalled, as we flew over Llandudno (which takes its water supply from the Black Lake), how in the old grammar school there (recent rubble rebuilt on now), in the sixth form, I had become infatuated by Charles Baudelaire's poetry of the voyage. His lines that tell of the child who loves maps and prints, lines that exclaim how big the world is by the sharp light of a reading lamp, could themselves delay me for minutes on end, in a kind of melancholy distraction. Don't ask me why. Passions can't be explained. We come into the world as we are. My siblings haven't lived as I have done, remotely. Nor have they lived like each other.

Now, on this day, how small was the world from the air, how big it loomed in memory, how much detail and incident swarmed around that coast, those toy headlands and seaboard hills and limestone bluffs, woods, rivers and mountains, the territory of the Red Wood and seven tiny miles west of it, the Wooded Hill. My mind zoomed in and out, not just from my literal vantage point, in mid-air, but from another world and being, a world of other knowledges amassed and distances travelled without resting place, by one then nearly a sixty-year stranger: how many times removed? But still, for all that, I was unforgetting and vitally grounded there, though time is unforgiving. My mind's eye still searched there, compulsive in its quest, and my pulse quickened at sight and thought of that childhood country by the Irish Sea, the plot and ground of my first story. As I looked down on it, I saw it all in detail, in a myriad flash-backs. I saw at once how I'd write it, as a triptych comprising: The Red Wood, The Black Lake, and The Wooded Hill. Just as you may read it now, if you please.

THE RED WOOD

Lunch-hour was announced to our stretch of coast by a wartime siren sounding the all-clear. Not that it hadn't all been clear for some time now, along that coast over which you have just flown, surveying the known world.

These were the late forties and early fifties. The war was over. But nothing begins or ends at once. The war still pervaded our lives. We were the fruits of its supposed cessation, we children in our boom year. It left some of our number with mothers only. One or two of us, seeming fatherless, were said to be half American, for our trouble. Here was one, they said, in the language of that era, with a touch of the tar brush. Though we thought nothing of that. Except I remember fascination, as to darker skin that darkened to brown in the summer, not freckled and tinder-quick to scorch red and peel, like my own epidermis.

A great horde of children we were, spawned in careless hope and joy at last, to fill the village with vigorous new life.

★ ★ ★

That siren wailing from Laundry Hill, on the outskirts of the Bay, seemed to make your tummy rumble, it was so well timed. The workers at the laundry dispersed home. A mile or so away in Pa D's Primary we must wait a little longer for a second all-clear, the school bell, a large hand-bell shaken along the corridor. But the siren whetted our appetites and primed us.

Now, when I think back to it, among the many echoes in my mind from wartime news footage, blitz-time movies and so on, the eerie siren-noise feels like the key to Belsen, shutter-gate to a hell of harrowing reels of celluloid... wailing, wailing... to a hell that had been visited on my parents' generation, all over Europe. But we took the Laundry Hill siren in our childish stride. It was just a normal part of daily life, blaring out, winding itself up and winding itself down, an inhalation and a sigh, to let us know lunch wasn't far away.

I suppose it was half-a-mile or so, for me, downhill and over Colwyn stream in Llawr Pentre. Then uphill I'd hurry past the terraced houses of Pen-y-Bryn and Edwards-the-blacksmith and horse-dealer's forge, and round the back of Ratcliffe's Engineering Works through the Fairy Glen, past Willy Winky the gardener's shed, across the little stream and through among the trees and shrubs, to 'Thornfield' on the Red Wood road. A place of cackling jackdaws and whistling songbirds and whisper and rush of Colwyn stream from the bosky Denbighshire back country.

At 'Thornfield', 'Workers' Playtime' would be on the Wireless, or 'Have a Go' ('Give him the money, Mabel'), and the News, read in a patrician voice that spoke from London. What a world it was in which only the lower classes had accents. Know your place. Hence the Elocution Lesson. As my sister knew, being surely one of the last girls in Wales to graduate in received pronunciation, at the end of an era. As I knew, corrected by my parents when, deliberately erring to test them, I'd pronounce 'lorry' as 'lurry', in the local manner.

Even as a young child I tried them consciously. I resented keeping two worlds between home and the Red

Wood road. The idea was, I suppose, for us all to sound like news readers or those women who sold cake-mixes or appliances, the first white goods, on the first television adverts, obscure relations of the queen of England, but sexually charged, as queerly they were. A strange world indeed, and yet it was a shadow of what it had been fifty years before, before both wars. Tug your forelock if you please. Know your betters.

Not that I don't know mine. How can you put pen to paper and not? How can you read the great writings spawned in our unnameable archipelago and not know your place? You are not on time's radar. Believe me, but give voice, as the songbird does careless of its doom.

But still, look sharp... it's 1953. Here comes Captain Miller with his pepper and salt moustache, and all the men on the road, one way or another, touching their hats or caps to my mother. Here's Mr Edwards the quarryman upright as a sledgehammer shaft, in his Sunday black bowler off to Church (Church in Wales). A nod and gesture with one hand at the rim. Look lively... 'A peach' the men at Ratcliffe's called her.

There must have been a day when the lunchtime siren wailed no more. But I don't remember it. Nor do I know when, if ever, as a small child, I connected its haunting cry with the war, the war that also marked our lives in other ways: rationing of meat, butter, eggs, sugar, soap... sweets... other essentials, in our 'Food Control Area'. Covered lorries in convoy trundled through the village. National Service soldiers in the back of them wolf-whistled at my mother, on their way to Kinmel Camp. Snub Meteors and box-like De Havilland jet planes soared greyly across the cold-war sky above. Now and then on a fine day we might see an Atomic cloud, mushroom beyond Pentr'uchaf or above the schoolyard, or out at sea, and pretend the end of the world was coming our way. Take a deep breath. Climb inside a brown paper-bag.... It was no age of innocence, but we at least possessed the innocence of childhood, happily murky with sin though we were, from the day we were born, in Calvinistic Wales.

What else could we be? 'Give us a *sws*,' said Gwyneth to me, and I knew why I loved her chestnut hair, her cool white cheek, and something in me stirring, to record that moment in my head for ever. Give her a kiss? We were with our mothers. I didn't want to, and I did.

We had no television in our house while we lived in the village, all the first thirteen years of my life that is, and we went to the pictures rarely, perhaps once every school holiday, or twice in summer. This made the local picture-houses – The Odeon, The Cosy, The Supreme – all the more places of romance and allure. (Not to forget the pastoral Arcadia where, one season, the new-sprung Teddy Boys ripped up seats and scandalised the citizenry, in a wild Presley frenzy, about 'Jailhouse Rock', was it? I think so.) Not having television at home turned watching 'The Cisco Kid' and 'The Lone Ranger' at my best friend Dick's house into stolen delight cut short, to be home in time for tea, six doors down the road.

What other trespasses and scrapes too there were to be had with Dick, whose family owned a butcher's shop: Dick and his mongrel cur Rinty, the most marvellous of mates, nervous as a bird, brave as a lion, and fit as a butcher's dog. Together we did things 'Thornfield' wouldn't have conscienced for a minute, building and maintaining an underground trench at the top end of their terrace, with a fire, and no smoke without one, and Woodbines to cough over and Player's Weights, cooking twists of flour and water.

Fearless, we'd drag sheets of corrugated iron, old carpets and linoleum scrounged from the tip at Fairmount, down the Muddy Path (past Captain Miller's allotment), and on up the Red Wood road, beyond 'Thornfield', to Dick's nameless house, to make our subterranean hide-away. There his mother turned a blind eye. She even dished up custom-made chipolatas to sustain us, out of a black and spitting frying pan, dark and rich sausages, full of meat, of a kind you could never buy over the counter, homemade for the family. Unless we drove her into a fury, as we did when we stole a bag of cement from the coal hole, with a view to making our trench a more robust and permanent fixture. The bag tore before we could lug it a couple of steps up out of the yard and cement powder went everywhere to betray us, blowing onto the washing, cementing our fate.

As to sausages, you never even dreamt of their like, with Daddy's or HP sauce. And no baked beans, as Dick, being too polite to say he didn't like them, once secreted into his trouser pocket, during tea at 'Thornfield'. He did so by a sleight of hand so deft as to remain to this day a marvel of the known world. Yet he never received the credit he was due. Unlike his sister who could eat a cream cracker without making a crumb. As their mother liked to say, by way of reproaching her son. How do you get baked beans-on-toast into your trouser pocket – short trousers, plump legs, tight pockets – while sitting at the table in full sight of everyone, without leaving a trace of sauce anywhere? By dint of genius.

And there'd be jelly-sponge for tea of inimitable flavour, and sloppy blancmange by the bucket. Dick's mother insisted on bringing blancmange down the road to 'Thornfield', in a big bowl covered with a dish-cloth, to shovel into Dick when he came to tea. She brought a table-spoon with her for the job. There Dick would sit being crammed with pink blancmange like a *paté de foie-gras* goose fattening for the slaughter.

You might one day expect to see him displayed in the window at the shop, all gooseflesh. 'Ripe young boy – home-killed. 1s 6d a pound.' '*Paté de blancmange.* 2s a pot.' Undaunted by our mother, his mother stood over him, in her wrap-around floral apron (in summer), or her broad-belted brown gaberdine (in winter wind and rain), to the last mouthful. Just so one day she brought an ugly old hedgehog on a shovel to show my mother the new family pet. It was a world, full of eccentricity, of ordinary folk and simpletons and oddities, and community.

There was, for a sublime example, the lady who whistled through her teeth. Every time she spoke, she whistled, like a twittering canary. We were once in the queue behind her at Trelevan Jones the baker. She had a cardboard box on the counter containing a large order of loaves. 'What's in the box? What's in the box?' I demanded loudly of my mother every time the lady whistled. Each time I asked Mrs Whitworth serving the canary-woman died of trying not to laugh. 'What's in the box?' I was convinced it was a canary. My grandad had a canary called Hamish. I knew what canaries sounded like. 'Shush! Shush!' said my mother, bending confidentially, and 'SHUSH!' for all to hear.

There was Alan in the terrace just below Ratcliffe's. He stood in the window all day knitting a scarf from a ball of wool that tumbled slowly as it unwound in a tall glass vase. How long *was* that scarf, where did it wind to in Alan's head? Up into the attic or the boxroom, like an anaconda, taking over the house. He seemed to have no other sense of time passing than the slow unwinding of a ball of wool.

While Sam Cook has it on his hands, and all the dirt of ages. Sam is Dick's nextdoor neighbour, and Alan-the-knitting's chaperone. He gives Alan his daily constitutional, an act of simple kindness. Sam owns houses on Beach Road. Rentier, rent-collector, and great unwashed, he's a short round man in a peaked cap and national health specs, with a moustache like a tired yard-brush and finger-nails like a badger's.

Don't let him give you a sugared almond out of his coat pocket. It's been there since before the war. Or that apple. Watch your mother snatch it away, with a set smile, before it gets to your lips. But if you are dutiful in pursuit of sixpence, go and sit an hour with Miss Cook, Sam's bedridden sister, and suffer her to teach you how to knit 'pan-scrubs' (pronounced with a strong Northern English accent), out of a wool wound with a fine wire.

What's the time? Only two minutes older than when you wondered last. Oh the sickly sweet smell of a bedridden body in a white mop cap and a shawl. Oh the race down the road after, clearing your lungs of mothballs and disinfectant, and the smell of fish and chips from Oldham's to greet you, and a waft of beer from the Ship nextdoor, the salt sea blowing beyond Min-y-Don, and the Emerald Isle Express snorting steam and soot, rattling along, laden with Irishmen, bound for Holyhead or Euston, the fireman in his shiny peaked cap, waving, as if it was all a novelty. For so life seemed.

If not at the pictures, where else might I have heard the siren, whether the air-raid warning or all-clear, except, perhaps, on the radio? Maybe parents explained or older children told us what it was. But I suspect no one told anyone. It was on the air we breathed. Yet I know, to me, it was the all-clear, not the air-raid warning. As who would need warning of lunch, unless they took school dinners? To be clear to go was what I wanted, back into momentary freedom, however fleeting; and fleet-of-foot I'd run to make the most of it, home to 'Thornfield', our damp little, narrow little three-bedroom semi with its short backyard and long steep garden terraced high above it, from which you could see the tops of the trees in the Fairy Glen, across the Red Wood road below.

But how keen I'd been to surrender my freedom to the prison-house of Pa-D's Primary. I suppose I adored my sister, or else envied her, or was merely very foolish and didn't know myself by heart. At any rate, when she went to school I missed her, and I thought I should go with her too. I began to clamour to go to school. As seems incredible now, to one for whom school days were ever and always the worst days of my life, early and late, kow-towing to petty authority, learning things I never needed to know and not learning things I did, the history of an education for most of the population. But I didn't want to be left at home. I thought I was missing out. (There's one born every minute.)

So an arrangement was made and I was allowed to go. I started school in my fourth year, the due age being five. But it was a disaster, even in the shelter of the beginning infants. I could not bear it. It seemed I was a very nervous infant, not cut out for a career in the infantry. What's more I was an embarrassment to my sister. She had to stand and hold my hand in the playground, waiting for the bell (ask not for whom it tolls: it tolled for me), where the infants ran on the girls' side of the hall. For boys and girls were otherwise segregated at play. This was not a good start for a boy, a damaging legacy, a telling indicator?

I'd got 'run down' as they used to say, in that now distant world of Cod Liver Oil, Radio Malt, Virol, Minidex, and other proprietary medications, intended to put iron in the soul, treatments so numerous that being 'run down' must have been a national pastime in those days. In my case it was to do with nerves, the nervous system. I was 'highly strung' as they still say of horses and used to say of children. I suppose this would be why Elliman's Horse Rub or

Universal Embrocation was also applied to me, from time to time, and other potions, on bits of greaseproof paper, on my chest, Wych-Hazel another I seem to remember, not to mention the consumption of Hot Toddy, my father's dire all-purpose concoction that might have put me off whisky for life, had I been less the man I am. So much do I have to thank him for.

In response to the stress of encountering school, I developed a large scab on my bottom, as the polite expression was, necessitating sun-lamp treatment, at Dr Miller's in the Bay. I remember the pleasant trips there to the West End on the top of the bus with my mother, and lying on the bed, under the big round Sun Lamp, and hearing my mother in another room, talking with Dr Miller, the family doctor, a Scot who drove a red Aston-Martin and between surgeries spent most of his time playing golf. Apart from my condition they'd perhaps be discussing my father's latest psychosomatic tummy and self-prescribed fish-diet regimen.

I had to be withdrawn. School fell back below the horizon. But I knew it existed now, and what it was, in all its horror, even when I wasn't looking at it. I was that much less innocent now. Time acquired new meaning, for it would run out. But however shadowed by experience, I had to return to the womb of home and discover myself again, in childhood's dreamy world, digging for coal on the top terrace beyond the gooseberry patch, among the blackcurrants, driving dinky cars through the mud, flying little silver 'Meteors' and 'Canberras' at arm's length across the sky, that manner of diversion, or sailing to and fro on the swing, all the world below me, dreaming along. I liked my own company but I had a convivial sense of fun too and knew a joke when I spotted one. (When I burped at table, 'just testing my brakes' I'd declare. Oh the age of the motor car....)

Once, up there at the top of the garden, I heard my father in conversation with Stan Valentine over the hedge. Stan was the black-sheep brother of the great Welsh Nationalist Lewis Valentine. It was said that as an infant he was so wilful his mother threw him to the end of the bed. Whatever that meant. Welsh was his first language. He liked to say in exclamation, 'Well, I'll go to the foot of our stairs!' He was this day sprinkling thick black soot from the chimney round his gooseberry bushes, to deter slugs and snails. My father, playing gooseberry to his neighbour's peace and quiet, was interested.

'Let me have some,' he said, 'I'll sprinkle a little on myself.'

At which, as if hand over mouth not to laugh aloud, I tripped rapidly down the steep concrete steps (how many, 39? – dozens and dozens, anyway it always seemed) wellingtons flapping, to tell my mother, about my father, the thought of him sprinkling soot over himself too much to bear. Humorous in my way I was, but also it seems nervous and prone to stresses and anxieties.

Not I think that I was especially sickly, not in any romantic way, you understand, as might have been interesting. But writing about this faltering exposure to schooling reminds me quite strongly of unlocated spells spent 'ill' at home at 'Thornfield', long afternoons, for some reason in my parents' bed, presumably for the view that my little back room didn't have, staring at the bare wintry tree-tops in the Glen, listening to the homely cackling of the jackdaws, on long interminable afternoons, pricking up my ears at hearing Mr James with his pony and trap come down the road at a trot, carrying milk churns to the dairy, from Pentr'uchaf.

I'd shoot out of bed when I heard the hooves and watch him go. He was a man you'd know now as one straight out of R.S. Thomas's early poems, a Lloyd George thatch of grey hair under his tilted cap, old trench-coat tied at the waist with regulatory binder twine. He was Iago Prytherch. I'd seen him up at the farm when I went to play with the Roberts brothers, red-haired Welsh boys in Red Wood country, and to lean over the sty to see and get a closer whiff of the *mochyns*.

Or it would be Hughie Bach, the casual farmhand, with the emphasis on casual, staggering up from the Ship. Drunk as a lord he'd struggle along, heading for the hills, for whichever farm outbuilding he spent his nights in. You'd hear him singing, or calling out, and he was a sight to watch, trying to snatch his cap up from the reeling road, singing in Welsh, earth of the earth. He made you nervous if you met him on his way but he was harmless they said, with quick but gentle hazel eyes. It always intrigued me what kind of being he was, another one who wore a belt of binder twine. A character they said, a rogue, handing his way up the road by means of the Glen railings, rolling and pitching, slumping, as if still aboard the Ship and the Ship at sea in wild weather.

During the war Hughie once tried to sell my parents a stolen goose from under his coat at the door. 'Iss a fine goose,' he said, flashing it out from the skirt of his coat. But they were having none of it. They knew whose goose it was. The story of his crime had run ahead of him and lay in wait to send him 'down the line' for a spell in Liverpool's Walton Jail. Another time he took my father for a ride, up in the back lanes after nightfall, near Llanelian, selling him a sack of black-market mud and stones, with just a foot of so of potatoes on top for good luck. Sometimes on a wet day you'd see him in a hood improvised from a sack, one corner poked into the other, with the rest of the sack hanging behind, keeping his shoulders dry. He always made you think of the earth, smell the earth when you saw him.

I was once brought to a sudden halt running in the Glen when round the corner I came face to face with Hughie Bach's arse, as he bent double to relieve himself, barely screened by a laurel, trousers round his knees. I doubt you ever saw anyone turn whiter in the face, whiter than Hughie's grey-pink arse, for sure, or beat a hastier retreat than I did that afternoon.

Or else it was the clopping laundry van, from Laundry Hill. For there were people in our lower middle-class ranks who used the services of the laundry. A sometime Lord Mayor, Mr Dunwell, Royal Welch Fusilier veteran of the Great War, lived two doors down, a Yorkshireman by birth. And there was Captain Miller, risen from the ranks, still further down, with his very pretty wife 'like an actress', and the Isherwoods, the McCleans and Miss Burke. These were people of standing, you'd think, but no one thought so, unless themselves. Mr McClean was a retired solicitor. He knew eminent men in London, just a little perhaps. The Isherwoods went into formal mourning, and closed their curtains, when the King died (as the entire road did for any neighbour's funeral). Yet young Miss Isherwood would collect bets from Walter Price, always at night, in a huddle at the front door, for a book someone kept, perhaps her mother or her dad? Or was she placing them?

'Have you heard the news?' What was it? 'The King is dead!' she whispered to my mother, in loud reverence, on the Abergele Road, and the man barely cold in his winding sheet.

The horse age had now all but become the race-horse age. But my father knew working horses and had worked with them, had driven a pony and trap, as a matter of course. It was a horse, the red horse Fox, from Bill Davies's stables in the uplands of the Bay, that nearly brought my story to an early close, at the tender age of nine. Fox bolted with me one Saturday morning, onto a metalled road and after about a quarter of a mile, off I came, knocking myself spark out against the bottom of a lamp post. The people who found me knew me and brought me home concussed and semi-conscious. I remember coming round and being sick into the sink all over the washing-up. Everyone on the Red Wood Road knew about it before I got home, from Dick and from my sister. Was I dead? Would I live?

Perhaps it was the protracted convalescence from this concussive episode and the resulting great span of time off school that makes those afternoons in my parents' bed seem both numerous and haunting, lying there listening out for the now nightmare tattoo of hoof-beats, gazing into the wintry sky, that was always so buoyant, because of the sea nearby. The sea ran not much more than half a mile away from our door, the white-horse sea. It would flood my mind forever, as a prospect of elsewhere, a restless realm of tides and skies and light, its light always there, in our daily lives, conditioning us, whoever we were, whatever our capacity for dreaming. Neptune tapped a rock and up sprang a horse. I saw the sea and my heart rode away. So it rides now at the drop of a hat, not for escape, but for respite.

Mr Edwards the smith (whose wife once described my father as 'very athletic', mystifying us forever) was largely a wrought-iron and an agricultural repair man now. But he shod horses still, and he rounded wild ponies up and held them, at the back end of the year, corralled at the old mill, to what end, I don't know. (The Belgian meat market they said at Price the Butcher.) One misty morning I remember coming up early from the shore by Pen-y-Bryn and seeing what seemed like hundreds of wild ponies off the moor herded together there. The uncommon mist that shrouded the village must have magnified my sense of their number. They stood shoulder to shoulder, packed, crowding the yard and up the length of the track from the mill to the road.

I would have been twelve, going on thirteen at most the time I saw them. I'd been down fishing in the early morning, attending a nightline, digging bait, one or other, or all three. The ponies all rough and ragged seemed like an apparition, a ghostly vision, neither neighing nor whinny-ing, in the great, still silence of the mist. Some of them had hooves like hockey sticks, from being on the moor and mountainside, with no hard surface under them to keep their toes in shape. It's a strange sight to see, a horse with all four hooves that way, like some mad attempt by Leonardo da Vinci to design a rocking horse or a mount for a horse-back ball-game.

It might have been the tail-end of the horse age, but still there were very few cars in our world at that time. Only Mr Pierce and Ernie Thomas owned a car on our road at the start, and Mr Meredith (of Meredith & Kirkham garage, so he hardly counted). If I remember right, even by 1956 and Suez there only one or two more; Suez an event I recall, not of course as 'Suez' but as something worrying, like Hungary and dark night images on the television news, chez Dick.

I always associate Suez with a grave conversation that passed in the road between Mr Pierce and my father, about petrol rationing. Mr Pierce was peering under the bonnet of his black Ford Prefect, or was it a Poplar? – I don't think a Pilot – a model on which the bonnet lifted and folded up from the side, as I recall, like a wing. How many horse power did it have? My father peered in with him as if to see. Then the two men stood up and talked, let's suppose, as would be likely, something about Nasser, and Eden's fallen world. What I do know is you'd have thought the end of the world was round the corner, running on empty, stuttering to a halt, the way Mr Pierce folded the bonnet down and closed the engine away, as if, it now seems to me, seeing him again in my mind's eye, consigning the car to the scrapheap for eternity.

My Scottish grandpa had a car, an old Austin with a crank handle, leather seats, and running boards. So far away was the world then he would sit me between his arms and let me 'drive' around the village sometimes, when he and granny came over on Sunday. Our own first car was called a brake, an Austin van with seats in the back and windows cut in the side, and minimal comfort. I think we must have had it in coronation year, or just before, from the proceeds of my father's writing, I guess. Whenever it was it was by 1954, when my brother was born. I remember father lying on the sofa in the rarely used front room, holding his brow because he found the car hard to drive. It wasn't that he'd never taken a test, which he hadn't, but that the brake had a novel gear-shift, fixed to the steering-wheel column, and he couldn't get the hang of it.

Cars were rarely left on the road but parked or garaged elsewhere, most of the houses on our road having no such luxury as a garage. My father rented a garage from an old lady, beyond Fairmount. He lavished care on his vehicle there, sealing its underneath with some kind of bitumen and wrapping its suspension springs with coarse tape coated with a stiff gluey-green-grey paste. One of his many mad precautions in life, this one I suppose to guard against corrosive salt air from the sea. I remember standing around all morning while he struggled and swore under the car applying the sticky tape. A cold dull morning but never quite boring because my father's antics always set such occasions on edge.

Pa D the primary school headmaster had a car, and my father's bosses too, at Ratcliffe's Engineering Company, some four hundred yards back down the Red Wood road from 'Thornfield'. They had very big and powerful cars and conceit to go with them. Thick-headed petty fat-cats they were, lunching at the Metropole, height of sophistication, in the Bay, on the spoils of war.

The war, the war.... We lingered in its aftermath. It lingered in our young lives. Even more than forty years on there was the war still. As when my nephew, a small toddling boy, halted outside Hughie Jones's house and called down the path to him a childish enquiry, 'Where's your gate?' 'They took it for the war,' answered Hughie, so many years later. (Never brought it back.) There was National Service too. I suppose that was what took Ernie Davies's son away. I remember him coming into our backyard in his uniform, boots and puttees, and giving me a Royal Welch Fusiliers cap badge. There was Korea, the Mau Mau, Suez and Hungary, Malaya, Ireland... so the never-ending war ran on, as perhaps Mr Farrell at the Laundry wanted to remind us: war as much a precondition of our existence as sex. Once in this time an IRA bomb went off at Kinmel Army Camp, not so far from us. I remember the shock of it – not of the bomb going off – but of the event as gossip.

I missed National Service by a good margin. But soon time came round as time will and I must enlist in the infantry again and face the world, and quite soon experience it as represented by the fanatical Pa D.

It must be said that such a world as Pa D made would be a national scandal, and illegal, today. For us it was a wild drama, violent, and comic too, in a grim way. But we weren't censorious. We thought it was just life and nowhere worse or better. It was all we knew. Fortunately for the infants they did not share the daily ritual of morning assembly with the upper school. They were sheltered from it for a couple of years, the better to render them ripe for the shock of first encounter. Little by little they soaked up rumour and tasted anxiety. In the infants life was gentle enough, though they struggled with me, for a while, trying to make me use scissors in my right-hand, but I am left-handed, and a pencil. How Miss Lewis pounded me in the back when I broke the pencil.

They picked me to play Joseph in the nativity. It doesn't get more innocent than that, and a very unlikely choice, to pick a nervous boy. So nervous was I that I not only knew my own part by heart, I knew everyone else's. When my mother rehearsed me, to try to build up my confidence, I would repeat my opening lines, and add: 'Then Mary says.... Then the First Shepherd says.... Then I say.... Then the Second or the First or the Third Wise Man says...' and so on and on until they'd all had their say and the Christ child came once again to Colwyn. The best Joseph they ever had, they said, as they always said. Be-robed in my sister's dressing gown, it was my only thespian triumph ever and (barring one other much later, in Synge's *Riders to the Sea*) the only time I trod the boards in my life.

They were the boards in the big Assembly Hall, which doubled for school dinners as a canteen. They were the boards on which each morning mad Pa D stalked into the limelight of his megalomania, and, usually, if not quite every day, lost the plot, or found the plot, perhaps I should say, his crazy version of it anyway. He was a short man with a short fuse, and vigorous in manner, made somehow more menacing by heavy black-framed spectacles. His white hair combed back from his hairline was wavy and, though fine, could seem unruly, as became a maestro.

Pa D generally wore a three-piece suit (in the summer a cream or sometimes a buff linen jacket). When he was really getting going he'd take off his jacket and conduct in his waistcoat. The sleeves of his shirt billowed, held fast above the elbow by little silver elasticated armbands. I can remember detachedly studying his dress, his manner, his frantic enthusiasm. It was as if I saw into his absurdity even then, his not being a man, but a schoolmaster, a particular kind of aberration, a king, a tyrant over children under eleven. My father detested schoolmasters and often voiced his scorn for the breed. Perhaps it was this encouraged me to observe Pa D critically.

But parents respected Pa D, my own included. He was energetic and well-intentioned, and saw above the horizon and beyond it, they would later say. They liked him very much. As to that horizon, Pa D once took a party of us by train to Bristol, and a coach to Wells to see the Cathedral and to the Cheddar Gorge, an old steam-train marathon, 6am to late at night. It still hangs in my mind, staring in wonder at the unknown world from that train. Perhaps I registered then the first pull, the first urge to escape that would later get the better of me, never say worst.

We sang hymns in the morning and some afternoons we'd be assembled again, for more of the same, and for musical, and once in a way, theatrical, education and diversion. A Shakespearean actor came one afternoon, all violet tinted make-up and period costume, discernibly a quare fella, even to my childish gaze, lisping speeches from Shakespeare, as if we understood a word, or knew what he was doing, or why. Yet I remember him so well I can see him now, delivering bits of Falstaff and Lear, as now I realise they must have been. We'd be played 78s of Kathleen Ferrier, the English contralto, while Pa D waxed lyrical and incomprehensible to us about the beauty of her voice.

Nineteen-fifty-three was quite a year, Coronation year, when we lined up along the Abergele Road clutching our coronation mugs, waiting on her majesty's majestic progress to wave our flags and cheer. There was bunting hung along a stretch of the road in the village, along the viaduct. I do remember catching sight of the queen and the duke beside her, on that bleak day, a very dull and chilly day. I was stood just below Rose Walk, opposite W.H. Smith's. I don't know what I'd expected but they struck me as too ordinary. They might have been anyone. I can still see them, and the open-backed limousine disappearing. My mother was up at Hebron on the hill, where there was no crowd, but just a few folk gathered. They stepped out into the road as the cortege approached and cheered, involuntarily, having vowed they'd do no such thing. She says the Queen wore pink, a pink hat, and they 'both looked beautiful'. Somehow I remain certain I glimpsed the queen in yellow, but from my height, peeping from the crowd perhaps I saw nothing at all, but the hood, like a pram-hood lowered at the back of the limousine, and the back of the Duke's little head.

In a world where news was so thinly broadcast, compared with the 24/7 wall-to-wall of today, we had no other view of it than what we saw with our own eyes and what we were told at home and school, about the Queen. In my case, if I heard it from my father, it would not have been enthusiastic. He disliked the idea of monarchy.

It was also the year Dylan Thomas died, far from his native country, an occasion of great sadness my parents felt. My father loved his stories. It was Dylan Thomas described the way we lived on the Red Wood road and invented it too. But more important for Pa D, 1953 was the year Kathleen Ferrier died. She died of cancer. No doubt he told us that too. It was my first year under his regime. What we were supposed to make of it I don't know, but some time later we were assembled one afternoon for a kind of memorial service to the great singer, in which recordings were played on a gramophone. These cultural afternoons were never, as

I remember, quite as fraught as, most days, the morning assembly proved to be, but they too could be the scene of sudden public canings.

We sang in English and we sang in Welsh, and also, sometimes 'Non nobis domine...' etc, in Latin, and not always hymns. Pa D loved music, with a vengeance, the vengeance being visited on us. He did the thing properly, conducting us with a real 'ivory' baton. If we started at 9am, it was not unheard of for us to be still at it at 11.30am, and not to be dislodged but by protesting dinner ladies anticipating the siren. 'Who is Sylvia, what is she?...' we'd warble, curious indeed as to who she might be. Sorry to know it wasn't Sylvia Hughes. Our ranks might be thinned, as one or other Sylvia fainted, thudding down onto the rough wood floor, and our singing suspended while her body was removed. Or, after a boy was sick there was a hurried halt and fluster as one of the staff put sawdust down, tipping it from a galvanised bucket, to absorb the vomit. Those nearby stood clear, now feeling sick themselves, from the sweet scent of sick and resin.

So our ranks were thinned and not perfectly serried by the end of a session. Then, for catching Pa D's eye at the wrong moment, probably during the hymn 'There is a green hill far away', a boy would be ushered off and pushed behind the dinner service cupboard, with a gratuitous clip round the head from one of the masters to see him on his way, while the other teachers stood by the radiators to keep warm or leant back on the wall, inscrutable but righteous-seeming, their arms folded in front of them. We would sing, our voices somehow tensed and yet relieved, knowing there was a victim installed, behind the cupboard, either side of which hung down old blackout drapes, there in the dim light to await his master's pleasure.

This boy was almost always the one called Sellars, a

swarthy boy, with next to no forehead. Sellars came from beyond our catchment and seemed older than the other older boys. You never felt sure about him. He did daring things in the playground, to show off, like climbing drain pipes. He knew a place out of reach to the rest of us where, if you put your hand in, you received an electric shock. We regarded him with awe and honest incredulity when he showed us what it was like to reach up along a piece of gutter to where the shock was to be had.

When it came time for Sellars to leave the school, to move on to the Secondary Modern, his place as scapegoat was at once filled by a boy called Clarke. It was if they belonged to some special tribe of victims, Sellars and Clarke. I can hardly remember any other boy being sent behind the cupboard, to await the cane, the grand finale to the morning, and sometimes a vigorous ear-boxing and thumping about the stage, as a warm-up. Pa D loved a quick flurry. There was something in Sellars's look was like a red-rag to him. Oafishness I suppose, and being 'twp', that is, thick or stupid, in Welsh.

At first it was reassuring to know Sellars had come to school, or which of us might not escape a beating? But in time you learnt not to worry. You knew that it would never be you, but always Sellars or Clarke. Just now and then I dimly recall someone else would be given a trial, as if he was a promising footballer who might take Clarke's place in the team, once he transferred up the league, to the dignity of private canings at the secondary school. The spectacle and general atmosphere would sometimes provoke tears of fear in Dick. I'd be aware of them trickling down his fat red cheeks as he stood next to me anxiously wringing a sodden handkerchief in his hands, until at one year's start his parents transferred him to the school at Llysfaen, in the next parish.

By today's standards, it was a scandal that Pa D should ever have had tender minds and hearts in his charge, a mismatch from another era. But at least it exposed us to life with a kind of dramatic intensity that made it real, distinct and unforgettable as lessons largely were not, except insofar as we learnt by rote, 'times tables' especially. Compared with brutalities my father had grown up with, it was a Sunday school outing. Though I know nothing first hand about those. The nearest thing I ever came to Sunday school was a funeral when a governor of the school died. I was ten years old and select band of us were marched through the village to the funeral service up the hill at Hebron. There we sang the Welsh hymns for which we'd been at short notice furiously rehearsed.

It was my first experience of a funeral and just about any kind of religious service, for we were, or I was, ungodly, having not even been christened. My father was dead set against institutionalised religion. He'd had an excess of it beaten into his Scottish childhood. (My sister was christened, though, attended Sunday School and for a time joined the Band of Hope, a teetotal sect, purely for the social life....)

Here in the alien pale duck-egg-blue plastered and varnished Calvinistic-Methodist world of Hebron Chapel, I saw solemn blue-jowelled hatless men, and their wives, sisters, cousins – behatted bereaved women I didn't know from Eve, sobbing their hearts out, faces puddled with grief, as the interminable service progressed, and the fearful organ marched its funeral march, or soared to the heights with 'Bread of Heaven' in Welsh, and the Minister delivered his sermon-without-end, world without end, in rousing Welsh. And though I didn't know anything of the sort here I witnessed Wales at full-strength, no matter it was all but on its last legs, swaying to sing its praises to heaven.

Next door but one to 'Thornfield' on the way up was the Baptist minister's tied house. His world was even more dour than that at Hebron, and he was paid a dismal pittance. We knew well two tenants of that house, both lovable men. One of them, a young man called Maxwell spent a good deal of time talking with my father. In the end so persuasive did the conversation prove that Maxwell gave up his calling to become a schoolmaster. Schoolmaster prejudices notwithstanding, this move was regarded at 'Thornfield' as a great triumph over the forces of darkness, as personified by the chapel deacons who held their man to account as if they worked for the Kremlin, so deadly were their attentions, so vicious their powers to bring to book.

No translations were ever offered. I didn't understand them. But I loved the Welsh hymns best of all. It shows I didn't lack discernment, for nothing's more rousing than a Welsh hymn. But the test piece of test pieces for us at Pa D's was an English hymn, 'There is a green hill far away'. Sometimes we would spend an hour on it, while Pa D got more and more exercised about the fact that when we sang 'without a city wall', the emphasis was all wrong, reflecting of course our incomprehension: why mention the city wall if there wasn't one? Sellars was one thing, but that line could work like a madman's flash, a glint of lunacy, across Pa D's brain.

Up would come the vomit. Down the troops would go. Bash would go the baton on the lectern. And bash, until, one memorable morning, it broke, and for the following week a much cruder one was used, one you could hardly take seriously, a clumsy thing, not at all the fine white implement, with its pointed tip and little cork end for the maestro to grip, with which we were accustomed to be kept in time. (For some reason I can still see it very vividly even now. It's 'handle' was whipped with string, a couple of inches and varnished over.) Even if we managed to get the pitch of 'with-*out*' right, we had 'O, dearly, *dearly* has He loved' to come, and the intensity with which we were supposed to sing '*dearly*' always cost us dear. We were irredeemable and literally so, for we could never quite sustain the right number of 'e'-s in the line that bade us love Him too and trust 'in his redeeeeeeeeeeeeeeeeming blood'. Even if we did come at all close to it, nothing – not the wildest tantrum – could stop us next propelling ourselves at a gallop into the short last line 'And try His work to do', and so spoil everything.

In spite of it all, as I say, I liked – and I still like – hymn singing, the old hymns that is (however banal their words), and I loved Welsh hymns best of all. We weren't a Welsh family. With a name like ours, how could we be? But my sister and I were Welsh by birth, natives of the place, and my brother too when he joined us. While that counted for nothing among the locals, it would matter to the world beyond, the unknown world, in time, and mattered much to me.

Meanwhile the issue for us was that we weren't English. For my part what mattered was that I was Scottish. Though this wasn't simply true. My father was Scottish, my mother unmentionably English. I was a native of Wales. But under Scots law my father assured me I was Scottish. I knew I was Scottish when my grandpa and granny came, that was for sure. They spoke bagpipe music. My granny was a McDougall and a Munro, of Highland stock, and a Bruce (a very un-McDougall thing to be) if you went far enough down one line, and a Sinclair from Caithness. My grandpa was from Galloway and would have killed you if you called him Irish. But his mother was a McGarva and they came from Ireland. The McNeillies too were Irish in the long ago when Galloway was part of the gaelic speaking world, as was nowhere else in lowland Scotland. They came from Co. Antrim. Their name is anglicised it's said from Mac an Filidh, son of the poet or poets.

Having a Scottish (though by derivation an Irish) name was no disadvantage in Wales. But if you didn't speak Welsh they tended to call you English, a thing deeply offensive to me. Even as a boy of eight, or particularly as a boy of eight, I remember hating that, and hated not having been born in Scotland. Most people who knew anything, knew my father was a Scottish writer. I was *not* English. Pain of death to call me so.... Though the truth is I've always belonged nowhere, not even at home. I was and am merely a witness to what has passed for life about me.

I can be so precise about my age in this matter as in others because I was eight in August the year my brother was born in November. I remember sharply many things and matters from that time. It was a time when I stepped deeper into solitude. It was a time not too much later – the ten months from November 1954 to August 1955 – when my father, during a family holiday at Traeth Coch on Anglesey, saw into this isolation and sought to compensate by spending time with me. This included renting a clinker-built row boat with a Seagull outboard and taking me fishing off Traeth Coch – Red Shore or Beach – known also as 'Red Wharf Bay'.

At one wild moment he set me off alone at the helm, to circle the inlet on a quite choppy grey morning, and at frantic speed. The engine roared and I raced off, speeding between moored boats, the outboard blaring, and by sheer luck and hair's-breadth getting by, unable to slow down because I'd not been told how the Seagull worked. Round I came huddled in the stern, eight going on nine-years-old, or just nine going on ten, head-on for the shingle slope, and came to a crunching halt, safe and sound, and excited, the engine roaring away and churning the water so loud I could hardly make out my father's directions as to how to wring the Seagull's neck.

It was in that time he talked to me, as we rode up and down on the choppy sea failing to catch fish, how it was that I was Scottish, and had no need to worry as to that. But it did worry me. Whatever it was worried John Hughes in Pa D's primary that he had to lie to me and say he was born in Philadelphia, I don't know. But I lied to him back, in no uncertain terms.

As to the Welsh language, the disadvantage was that no one in the family knew any Welsh. Welsh lessons were always a great mystery and there was no one to turn to, and no one to mind what result you got. So scandalously low stood Welsh then, almost done for, as R.S. Thomas and others, like Lewis Valentine and Saunders Lewis knew. It was a national disgrace and those who were angry about it were right to be angry. They might have been a lot angrier and taken up arms like the Irish. But they worked largely by stealth in the end and by tongue and pen and modest protest won what is now beyond doubt one of the great cultural victories of our post-colonial times and no recent tally of dead to keep.

But I jump ahead; forget the Welsh language. Indeed most lessons were a great mystery to me, for quite a long time – for far longer than might be considered 'normal' or average. I had miserable difficulties learning. Perhaps I had what are now classed as 'learning difficulties'. At any rate, by any standard, I took a painful age to learn to read. I found it a mystery and I'm not sure why. I found it hard to connect words with their sounds. I looked at them and they seemed like objects to me, opaque combinations from the alphabet, attractive but meaningless, except I knew that they generally meant what you saw in the picture above them. As long as there weren't too many things to choose from, that was fine. Otherwise they swam before my gaze like fish in a tank. My progress was so slow that my father, an impatient, hot-tempered man, took an interest in it. He was like Pa D on the home front, without the cane, but with far greater intensity of rage and I suppose far more pervasive and intimate and so crueller authority.

What did I have in my head, sawdust? – he'd rant furiously. I am sure this helped a great deal. But help or no, my progress through the Beacon Reader series was painful. Book One about the wretched farmer 'Old Lob' had me dug in for the long haul and not just down to Christmas. I was like those soldiers in their trenches in the Great War. The longer it went on, the worse it got. The worse it got, the longer it went on. In the process I suffered a kind of educational shell-shock. As for arithmetic, I couldn't even begin to spell it. Nothing seemed to add up, except blushing and burning unhappiness, and fear.

Words swam before my gaze. They were like the perch my father kept in a fish tank in the backyard. Their world was a silent mouthing world. They couldn't say their letters either, but at least they were full of life and a different, an absorbing, mystery. I could stand and stare at them for half a morning at a time, feeding them earthworms and slaters and other grubs I found under stones, watching them dart and turn and vie with each other, bold, bright, green, dark barred, ruddy-finned, spiky hump-backs, darting over the gravel bed of the tank. The word for them: 'perch' – so odd after all, paradoxically sedentary, or more than five yards longer than any perch you saw. What sense is one to make of words? What not? The word is your oyster.

Then one winter the tank froze. The thaw came. The tank burst and the poor perch perished. Their silence now complete, they were like that 8lb pike my father caught and for half a day perhaps, but it seemed for ever, had hanging on a meat-hook from the cistern in the disused outside lavatory. It seemed to me that I peeped in at that door a thousand times to hear what the pike had to say out of his big unfunny grin – it would have been a she in fact, as the bigger pike are – a dark, browny fish the way an old one is, scales now dulled, eye set matt, before being cut up into lengths and cutlets. Pike a good word for a stiff fish, like a pikestaff. The pike I would know on the end of my line were greenish, barred and spotted, with pale bellies, lean young fish, not monsters. Though they spoke volumes to me, hooked from the Bladnoch below Crouse Farm, the Bladnoch in which it was said there were pike big enough to take the leg off a drowning horse.

I am now more or less as literate as the next person. I have earned my living scribbling, one way, or another, for most of my adult life: from births, marriages and deaths on local rags to national broadcasting, to the more extreme ends of pedantic scholarship. But beyond earning a living of sorts it could also be said I have lived for language and the word, quite wildly, to my cost now, as well as to my gain if not to my profit, more than most people I know, following my muse. For this reason this miserable period in my education intrigues me. It intrigues me all the more that when at last I started reading, sometime again when I was about eight, I did so as it were overnight, from nought to top speed. The thaw came and I was free at last. If only I'd been able to read earlier... and to have read Jean-Jacques Rousseau to boot. How I'd have rejoiced to concur with him that 'reading is the curse of childhood'.

So the age of eight was a turning point, a seamark in my voyage. What had been going on meanwhile? What had not been going on? I am an eye. Stare at the world. Stare at the word. What a queer thing it is. What a queer fish that one is.

What is it? A fish called 'perch'. What is it doing, especially in oh so mutable, compounding and confounding Welsh? *Draenogiad...* the word for perch fish, meaning: hedgehog head [– *draen* = thorn, *draenog* = hedgehog, *iad* = pate or skull or head]). *Penhwyad...* the word for pike, meaning: duck head [– *pen* = head, *hwyad* = duck]). How inspired that duck-head, how graphic and true. Don't ask me which tongue I'd prefer to think and live in. Duck-heads fond of a duckling dinner too.

Today I like my language textured and sprung. In poetry I like it to rhyme and half rhyme and alliterate and sing and delay about itself. Vertical a poem is and I like the path that winds down the mountain to go this way and that (as did John Donne, a Welshman some say, who profess to know), by way of vertiginous caesurae too. In prose also I want and need it to resist its horizontal, its linear path, to be rhythmic, and to hark back, with elliptical back-thraws, parenthetical whirlpools and eddies, bightsom in the aftergait, as Hugh MacDiarmid put it. So for as long as I can remember have I always.

I like to sound words with the eye. I still sometimes catch myself pausing, struck by their oddness, as if I've never seen them before. I don't say them audibly but say the words to myself as I read. Perhaps something in me wanted that then, or registered it even in such simple beginning phrases and sentences, and it got in the way of reading? Or perhaps it all was just delayed development of my wiring, complicated by attendant anxiety? Perhaps this preference for textured language is also a Welsh thing, a thing in my case derived from Welsh-in-English, partly alliterative, generally alien to English formations, with some residual trace about it that English is foreign in construction and sounding to the ear, if not in my case in vocabulary.

While I admire prose that's plain and even, simple,

unaccented, measured, disinterested, I do love it to be deep and crisp and uneven, energetic and opinionated. I hate safety-first. I like sentences to go off at a tangent, or to have a little touch of opacity bred of thought's resistance to the expected, like jack-frost at the window, denying transparency. Such as now no one in our lost archipelago knows anything about. So frost-proof has our centrally-heated world become, so uninflected, so flat, so bland. I nearly wrote illiterate. (I *will* write illiterate.)

How deprived you westerners and northerners are who have never woken to the ice fern-lands and frozen forests, the deep tundras, the Siberias in the window pane, as you take the temperature of the lino through your bare toes. Life should not be choked with cotton wool, as for the immortal wretched of the earth it is not. Stare at the word. What might it not do? What might you not do with it? Step up and speak. Spare not a thought for the chorus of doubt and disagreement or the disciples of perfection. All that will always look after itself.

Whatever the nature of my encounter with the word, the thing missing from the account is day-dreaming. All children are great daydreamers, their minds always at play. (What are you *being*?...What are you *being*? my two-and-a-half-year-old granddaughter demands excitedly to know of me, when I get down on all fours. A tiger, I decide, having up to that point thought I was being just myself.) For my part, when pushed and punished for my slowness, when struggling, I diluted my misery and confusion, and only made things worse, by deliberate day-dreaming. I threw the switch on my heart's ejector seat. My eyes skimmed off the page and my gaze turned inward in no time and I was away. The more I stared out the more I stared in. In fact day-dreaming has been my modus operandi ever since. Just so it invents this page with its illogical optimism and momentum, and air of necessity.

My father was fierce but only meant his cruelties in the heat of the moment. We had many and frequent stormy episodes, with him ranting and raging at something, an inability to read, a pair of new shoes scuffed and battered on their first day out, or the need for new shoes in the first place, as if you could help your feet growing, a terrible school report (very commonly in my case), something and nothing, money, and work, Ratcliffe's, and writing books, writing and writing in the middle of the family: hammer, hammer, hammer of the two-finger typewriter rattling and thumping and dancing a jig, as with a swipe he raced the carriage back, spawning millions of words, on the fold-down bureau, in the alcove under the hot-water tank, below the window, beside the backyard where with a rash kick of small hard ball I once shattered the glass about his head.

But I got off lightly. An evening huddled in the dark on the stairs, on the rust carpet, with mother failing again to pack our bags and leave. I had a friend for whom a broken window meant the strap and the wooden spoon on his legs and three or four hours in the 'spence', or under-stair cupboard, dark as a coalhole, and stale with the odour of town gas that hung about the meter. Nor did the boys I knew have a father who wrote stories you'd hear on the radio, one about a boy called Andrew, a man who wrote books and was, to a proud boy at least, different from everyone else, in this and many another respect. A man who loved the written word and loved no less to fish for trout.

But he did keep us a little strapped for cash. Not that we wanted for anything but that he made sure we did. These were the days in the lower middle classes of house-keeping money and the housewife, Monday washday, bubble-and squeak, Friday fish day, and penny-pinch through the week. As now seems glaringly clear, these were days in a system of oppression of women, and gross domestic injustice. If my mother found herself short, for whatever reason, she didn't dare ask for more. If she had no choice but to ask, because of some unlooked for necessity, she always paid the price, in reproach and blame.

Yet if he decided a new fishing rod, or some tackle, or other 'essential' purchase was called for, the new fishing rod was bought, money no object, and the best money could buy. Such things could be justified in that fishing took him to the wilderness. The wilderness was the icing on our cake. It did more than pay the bills, in that my father earned half his income, above what he earned at the engineering firm, writing about it, writing about the wilderness and the natural world. (In all he earned a thousand pounds a year in those days.)

They were not the good old days. No matter the war did more to liberate the people than acts of parliament ever managed (than anything since the previous calamity), they were still relatively mean old days of deep inequality among nations and races, classes and sexes. (Housekeepers and house parlourmaids wanted.) Narrowness and prudishness tended to prevail. A divorcée was a fallen woman, little better than a whore. They were quaint days too, comic now to look back to. Businesses advertised for smart van boys. Sales ladies were required – for confectionary (experienced) – permanent position if suitable. Permanent? A thirty-nine year-old 'gent' of smart appearance 'will do anything'. What does he have in mind? Not much. And down at the pier the comedy was the same, served up by the like of Ted Ray, Terry Thomas (so confidingly *intime*), Beryl Reid, Michael Bentine, Harry Secombe (I thought your father was going to die), Jimmy James and Norman Evans 'Over the Garden Wall' (...you can taste that cat in the custard).

If it seems quaint now, it seemed immortal reality then, like Bob Bananas in the Christmas pantomime, like Mr

Alcock's homemade ice-cream, and the question you loved as you drooled to watch him stack up the cone and round it and firm it into place, deftly, generously, with the back of his scoop: 'Any flavouring?' Flavouring being a kind of syrup, orange or strawberry, also used in milkshakes, that he'd drizzle over the ice, and you licked it before you were out of the shop, because it was so lovely. It was possible as a child to recognize the oddity of Mr Alcock, as clearly I did, for so I recall him, in his dairyman's white or some days buff coat, his little bit of a moustache, selling sweets and ice-cream, in a northern English accent. Two and fro he'd go between the shop and a kind of cold parlour backroom. But you didn't think of him as anything but a fixture in the world, a given, who'd always been there and always would be, in his little shop near the corner to school, on the Abergele Road, turning an honest penny.

In the fiscal regime my father oversaw, we McNeillie children had much less pocket money than most of our friends, with fewer and smaller increases. We made do. It was good for us. We weren't ground down as were many boys I knew at school, some of them heartbreakingly, living in post-war prefabs by the gasworks, fathers away, in the merchant marine or the forces, or just absent without leave. But to my shame I remember once at a hardware counter stealing a Christmas present for my father, for want of enough to buy a little green millstone, with a red handle and a bracket to fix it to a bench, having obtained from a bran-tub in the village hall, for all I had, bars of soap for my mother.

I found that millstone, still functional, the stone worn down low, among my father's tools, when he died. Like a ghost, the millstone round the neck of my childish guilt, stared at me, questioning my character.

So truth will out. And here it is, for a wonder, guilt become shame at last.

Once

★ ★ ★

When Matthew Arnold visited an Eisteddfod in Llandudno in the 1860s, he famously described our strip of coast as anglicised, and wrote off Wales to the east as not really Welsh. Among many another misjudgement in his outrageously imperialistic essay, this view was a travesty of Wales, even in Wales as I knew it, so many years later. For anglicised Wales was only a coastal ribbon of resort conurbation, half a mile thick, at the most. It's largely white-settler mentality was as ignorant as any to be found elsewhere across the Empire. But being on England's doorstep, it was all the more overpowering because not only was it deaf, it was also invisible to itself... as could not be said of arrangements in Asia or Africa. There at least the white man stands out like a sore thumb.

Truly Welsh Wales was a short walk up the Red Wood road, and Welsh life itself existed in the towns, like an urban fox, and however abused and mocked by incomers, and slighted by Whitehall, it held its ground, in chapels, in bilingual versatility, and would not die, though it was hard to see how it could live, and impossible except as a daydream to imagine it ever flourishing again as now it does, as not so much miraculously as by sustained dissent over centuries, quiet community, native wit, and at last the winds of change reaching home, having nowhere else to go.

Matthew Arnold had wanted to see the 'English wedge' driven into the heart of Welsh Wales. At the same time it was largely by his influence Celtic Studies came into being in Britain. He wanted Welsh to be a dead language, for academic study only. (Not that even the ancient dead languages are dead.) You can't be culturally murderous without being socially so, and why would anyone want to be?

In those days, just up the road and beyond in the heartlands of the north – away, too, among the London Welsh – the language was like Glyn Dŵr himself, always on the move, always there, unheard, unseen to the non-Welsh, like a well-kept secret. No matter periodically there were those who betrayed their compatriots in the name of an English tendency. Innumerable groups and organizations flourished to foster Welsh, ancient and modern: societies to nurture Welsh hymnody, singing festivals great and small, youth movements, eisteddfodau, local and national, for young and old. It was like religion and bound into religion still, as it had always been, since Elizabeth I commissioned a translation of the Bible into Welsh, perhaps the single act that did most in all history to keep the tongue alive.

Coed Coch Road in Welsh would be Ffordd Coed Coch (Road... Wood... Red), but it was a bilingual road in its denizens and knew it so. That's what it said on the sign. Even more than the all-clear it was a mystery. Who knew where the Red Wood stood? Was it the Fairy Glen? But the Fairy Glen was only at all red in autumn. Where was the Red Wood? In what way was it red? In a bloody way, as a site of battle in the long, long ago, some people have said, an encounter between Welsh and Saxon princes, Anarwd avenging the death of Rhodri Mawr against Athelstan of Mercia, or something of that sort, as could never be established, but might be true to the spirit and history of naming in that country. For sure, anyway, the estate of Coed Coch is on record back to 1246, exactly seven-hundred years to the year of my birth.

Of course, these weren't matters I dreamt of for a moment as a child. The beauty of childhood is that you don't know much and you don't know what's going on most of the time, because you're in a world of your own. Yet how vivid it was and enduring its experiences. How when you pause to examine incident and moment, sight and sound, they open up into detail to be reinvented.

I did come consciously to wonder once in a way about the wood being red and how it might be, and when I was a bit older I remember wanting to find it. I had only to cross the road to get into the Fairy Glen, which was at least a step in the right direction. A municipal garden in a dingle, the Glen was an arm of woodland tapering up into the country, carefully but not over-carefully tended and planted, with terraced paths, and Colwyn stream in summer burbling or in winter gushing brown at its foot. They'd created a diversion from the stream itself, higher up at the top of the Glen, to make a second shallow water-course, six or seven inches deep at most through most of its length, a foot and more at the sluice-gate where it began, crossed in three places by flat wooden footbridges. The little stream, as we called it, ran a few hundred yards beside the top terrace. It spilled down at last in a waterfall, back to rejoin its source, and flow round by Edwards' mill to the shore. Here were sycamores and elms, oaks and beeches, and lesser trees, conifers, shrubs of all sorts, yew trees, a run of cane along the upper stream, the occasional prickly berberis, a bank of trimmed laurel.

The Glen contained a whole world of hideouts and lurking places, for boys and nesting songbirds. Though it was tended by the little fat man we knew as Willie Winkie, it admitted wildness too. As long as we were back, or in sight, when we said we would be we could disappear there all day, if we wanted, playing at war and westerns, furtively curious about, but suspicious of girls, following and spying on courting couples, peeping through foliage, tracking and stalking Red Indian style.

Here I'd mooch alone down along the lower stream, setting lines for trout at evening, and sometimes catching them by the morning, sometimes catching eels. It's all run down now and you'd have a heart-attack if your eight-year-old, your ten-year-old disappeared into it for half a minute for fear you'd never see him or her alive again. (The place of harmless Willie Winkie with his padlocked hut, and of feral Hughie Bach, taken by the spectres of addiction and abduction now.) As for the delicate trout, the polluted stream probably gave them all heart attacks long ago.

As I grew older, I ventured beyond the Glen, by field and hedgerow, bird-nesting, in the lovely hilly countryside of what we knew then as Denbighshire. Then I might follow the feeder stream up beside Peulwys Lane and under the road, away into the woods and farmlands of Parciau, or in the other direction, up and along toward Pentr'uchaf, or far beyond, under the droning telephone wires, to Dolgau and to the Dolwen crossroad, or even to the hamlet of Dolwen itself, the ancient village of Llanelian too.

Here the hedges in the spring were full of songbirds: blackbirds, song-thrushes, dunnocks, chaffinches, green-finches, goldfinches, yellow-hammers, robins, wrens.... Here swooped the sparrow-hawk. Here the kestrel hung breathtaking in mid-air, preying on vole or mouse. Here on the telephone wire the yellow-hammer called for a little bit of bread and no cheese, and swallows twittered snatches of composition, minims and crotchets on a stave.

It was up in the direction of Dolwen you might see Miss Brodrick in her bowler hat, trotting in her trap, drawn by a white Welsh Cob, of which variety she was a world-famous breeder, out at Betws where she lived, at the big house of Coed Coch, a person of note. I remember my parents point-ing her out, as you might point out a rare bird, and a rare bird she was, with her sanguine cheeks and her black bowler. She owned Coed Coch... the Red Wood itself, wherever it was. Her white pony then would have been some descen-dant of 'Coed Coch Madog', if not the aging beast himself, a grandson of 'Coed Coch Glyndwr', legendary animals.

Once

★ ★ ★

The two hinges of the year, spring and autumn, are the sweetest, surely, when the door opens and closes, when change turns the heart on its axis. Climate change now necessitates the re-writing of everything. Annotation is required to know the shepherd's calendar, to know what March and April or October and November, Spring or Autumn, once meant to Edmund Spenser, John Keats or John Clare. But I still catch myself registering the aura of spring as I used to, foretasting it, in light as it lingers in a bare wood, loath to go under and earlier to rise. The little finger-hold of daylight clinging on beyond its time, before its time, the first of birdsong, sometimes misplaced, make me look up and look, now, in my sixtieth year, to those old-fashioned bird-nesting days when the carrion crow, inveterate egg-robber itself, began to mate and brood. It would sail in its windy crow's nest, come the end of March and early April, to hatch four or five blue-green eggs, magically blotched and spotted orangey-brown, way out on a limb. So the rook would rebuild, and the bare-knuckled hedges come into bud. What though that little light's probably an illusion now, some freak moment of false November or December?

Time comes round none the less, however out of joint the day, and the need to reproduce coursing in the blood prompts the birds to build and whistle and sing, cry or crow, mewl or honk, coo or quack, twitter or chirrup, as ever they did, since the start of time, proclaiming their territory. On such burgeoning mornings, to step out across the road to the Glen, and to wind up away on Dolwen or Llanelian hill, or the gorse-blowing Marian, the known world of Wales in view below, and sky swept cloudily grey, in downpour or in dry, and the sea running on the coast with its seascape sky, was a dream come true, a dream nurtured at bedtime and hatched once more with the day, head full of hedges and banks to comb and search, in vivid intimacy.

It was an education without the intervention of a master, an absorbing study of birdlife, habitats and habits, in my native heath. It was natural religion with yourself alone and the god-in-things to lift you and keep you, an outlaw now as you'd be, a wicked disgrace, a thief of those extraordinarily beautiful eggs, never quite the same in their markings even within species, from nest to nest.

So much that was possible then is impossible if not unimaginable now. So much that was legal then is now against the law, and if we broke the law in little ways, the law slept or turned a blind eye, and no harm done give or take a small egg, a speckled trout, an apple.... I remember how for a time we had a sawn-off double-barrelled four-ten shotgun in our possession, to a boy's eye a beautiful little weapon with hammers, like something in a Western. It was given to my father or lent, I don't know which, by the postman. He used it to shoot pheasants from his Royal Mail van as he did his rounds out in the back country.

It didn't seem at all a serious matter that the postman should behave in such a way, or that such a lethal and illegal weapon should come into my father's hands: so did barbed snatching hooks for taking salmon, and a barbed tine for spearing them, both with a socket that would fit on a hazel stick and a cord through a hole in the socket to draw it tight and secure it in place while you snatched or speared. So when you had cunningly done the deed you could dismantle your tackle, wrap the cord round it, and slip the incriminating device into your pocket and concentrate on hiding the fish.

I don't know when the concept of protected species

arrived, but it wasn't illegal, at least as far as we understood, to possess the blown eggs of wild birds. Game-birds I suppose were always off limits. Not that that deterred me, if I came on a hen pheasant incubating eggs in the bottom of a hedge. The bird might slip away, but an egg, if not too far gone, might be taken and blown. The whole clutch might well have been taken and eaten. I never did that but I'm sure that was not upon any principle, but a matter of fortune. The only eggs I gathered to eat were the herring gull's. The egg from which might have hatched the original English Chinese restaurant joke, only we had scarce a Chinese restaurant then, to wit: waiter, this egg is rubbery. And lovely-rubbery they were too.

I had inherited two boxes of the eggs of many species my father had collected as a boy and youth in Scotland. Just to prise the lid off those flat shortcake tins and gaze at the eggs in their partitioned squares and nests of cotton-wool was enough to inspire a hundred adventures, not least flights of fancy to North Clutag and to Galloway. But it wasn't possessing the eggs or adding ever rarer ones to a collection that really mattered, but discovering nests, stalking, observing the comings and goings of birds, their startled departures as you happen on them, their fearful or fearless sitting tight until you can all but touch them, the looping arrival of a greenfinch into a holly hedge and its circumspect diversions; to find a nest in process of being built, to watch as building materials, fine moss, slender grasses, a feather, mud, twig, shavings of silver birch bark like fine foil, are carried... where? Here... in this branching fork, this mossy nook or cranny, thorn thicket, eave or outhouse gable, limestone cliff-ledge, or without building at all on a sea-pink thrifty pebbled shore.

This was knowledge won with patience and it fostered intimacy of seeing and being, absorption into the world, one thing leading to another. There was you might say nothing to distinguish between a boy's eye and a bird's eye view for watchfulness, and time stood still, attention undivided. Though I think there was boredom involved too, of a unique order in rural life, not self-conscious like the town's *ennui*, but something integral to the whole, a form of biding time and being bound by it. Here life could seem all in-waiting, the known world too well-known, the horizon beyond reach, a prison, and time spent killing time, in the hours between tides, between dawn and dusk, when the best fish move, and life bestirs most.

I remember enough discoveries, enough arduous climbs and clamberings to fill a book with episodes. But would you want to climb through them, through a tangle of sentences, as up into the branches of a hawthorn you might struggle, torn and pricked, spiked hard suddenly in the top of your head, cut down your cheek, your knuckles raw, your limbs scratched and grazed as doggedly you ascend to worm a hand into a magpie's thorny, domed house, to retrieve an egg – sometimes a bluish egg, sometimes an olive one.

Now somehow slip it into your mouth and keep it float-ing safely there, safe from every jolt and slip, safe from filling your mouth with an explosion of egg and yolk and shell, the dry birdlime taste already there to spice it. Rather a dull egg for so much trouble. But I took the trouble, as if I knew I was stashing away meaning for my future self, but knowing nothing of the sort and never a second thought, the process of selving being predetermined.

You wouldn't want to follow, but follow me just this last step down under the high wooden bridge. Lower yourself carefully through the rails and pick your way down the slipway where Colwyn stream enters the Glen proper, to reach the grey wagtail's nest in a hole in the walled bank, a teaspoon tied to a stick to help you fish out your little speckly-marble egg, with its squiggle hair-line, not unlike the devil's signature on the egg of a yellow-hammer, but an obvious forgery.

The stream is loud and the light in the trees above and in the saplings, in the stone itself, seems to close round you. The stream is louder than usual. The wagtail calls from downstream, wagging and wagging. You can see it trying to distract you but you can only intermittently hear its clear note ring out against the rush of the stream. The water seems louder than usual today, and it is because there's been sudden subsidence since you came this way last year. Now there's a great rectangular hole in the slipway, perhaps twelve feet in length – and how many feet deep? – into which the stream plunges and accelerates, cold and seething, cut water, bravura. It amazes you to see such turbulence and distracts you as the wagtail failed to do, as a sixth sense tells you here is a place to come back to at once and to lay a line for a trout.

So one thing follows another, and off you go, and before the day's much older you are back with a few worms and a little number 12 hook on a length of nylon and a stone for anchor, and cord line to join your tackle to a secure place, carefully concealed in the ivy. The anchor twists and turns in the force of water, then finds a hold, and your bait hangs in the stream. There it swims to await your return, perhaps before evening has fallen, perhaps quite early next morning. Pull the line in to find a little trout on your hook, beautifully spotted and green-backed, luscent, and cream-bellied. Just stare at it there, as your mind takes its indelible snapshot impression, ever bright to see again, the speckled fish. And don't now forget the wagtail's nest, fish meanwhile for your pretty speckled egg as well.

Everything was inward and immediate, and called forth ingenuities. How did I know how close to hatching an egg might be, if I hadn't found the nest before the clutch was complete? By experience and guesswork, by the week of the month, by the parent bird's reluctance to desert, by holding it up to the light, weighing it in the palm, or, if the ditch nearby had water enough to support it, or if there was still-water anywhere near, by testing to see would the egg float, or sink. If it floated the embryo was too highly developed to blow it through the pinprick hole. Better put it back and hope for the best.

The conventional way to blow an egg free of its white and yolk was to prick a hole at either end, a hawthorn or a wild rose thorn from the hedge was handiest for pricking, and then to blow through it, from the rounder 'big-end' until its contents came out, over your fingers sometimes, over your chin if the wind blew, and sometimes back into your mouth. You could blow the eggs of larger species through a single hole about mid-way down the egg, through a fine straw or grass stalk. There was a coarse kind of grass you could find by the stream. Pull it and it came like a joint from its socket, and with a careful cut from your penknife you could get a treasured length of three or four inches with the finest bore to blow through.

You could wish for nothing better. But either method the hazards were the same. When what was in proved too thick to come out, you must blow harder, and the exertion might cause you to grip the egg too tight and so break it, especially if it was a small egg, like the delicate egg of a warbler, a whitethroat, a blackcap, or a wren, a dunnock or from up at the farm a swallow. Or you might suck the last of it out into your mouth. Or the embryo was too advanced to come out, or the egg was addled, a too-early egg, or the nest recently abandoned, perhaps because of prying boys, like that much coveted greenfinch's that you came upon too late.

There was a code, never to take more than one egg from

any nest. But two or three boys might together exceed it, boys being boys, nasty, brutish and short, with no savagery too base. So I remember being one of a righteous trio who found a young cuckoo in a dunnock's nest. The sight of the decayed corpses of its fellow nestlings on the ground being consumed by ants and other creatures, inspired collective indignation. Until, like a crowd that has worked itself up into beating someone to death, we removed the fat cuckoo chick from the nest and killed it. I will not name the boy who sat on it. But it was not I. I daresay I'd have killed it with a stick, or stamped on it. The RSPB would have found all three of us guilty. It didn't seem that way though. We weren't tender or squeamish. We were fighting the cause of the dunnock. But really we were murderous brutes.

★ ★ ★

As to tender or squeamish, I am sure there would be health and safety rules and regulations, and laws against it now, but in those early years, a special treat was to go with Dick's father in the back of the van to the slaughterhouse when he had business there.

The extended family had a farm at Llysfaen. Their best meat was home grown and killed just down the road at Abergele. I can remember wandering around the slaughter-house, while Dick's father attended to business. We'd see cattle shot with a bolt gun, great beasts toppling, suddenly weak at the knees, and sheep rolled onto a wooden cradle kicking their stiff legs as the gun was put to their heads. We saw their carcasses disembowelled – what a membrane sac a bowel is – steaming, hanging from hooks, all in a mayhem of bleating and lowing and bellowing and squealing and clatter and skid of hooves, and the shouts of men, and the rattle of crush bars and pens, and aisles, and urine, bowels and dung everywhere under foot and in the air, reeking healthily, before the purging hose.

It was life. It was everyday. So was the man in the basement back at the butcher's shop, sitting on a stool in his vest, under a bare light-bulb that dangled from a long flex, plucking away in a room caged off with wire netting, surrounded by feathers and Christmas chickens and turkeys. When he'd finished plucking one, he'd lunge, arms spread, to snatch up the next one and wring its neck, as we stood by, feathers billowing everywhere, and a sudden cacophony of gobbles and squawks and frenzy.

We'd watch the scene fascinated a while. It was like a sideshow in hell, down there in the dark cellerage. Once in a kind of dumbshow for our benefit, the man held up a plucked bird by the neck and easing his hand down its body to the rump, produced an egg. Either it was a fowl on the brink of laying, which is quite likely, or a clever bit of conjuring, if not as clever as Dick's baked-bean trick. As to the chicken and egg, I always believed my eyes, whereas with the baked beans, you couldn't, so fast Dick moved, defying time.

★ ★ ★

To everything its season. There were shoreline seasons too, and tidal passions that came to fill my waking thoughts, to distract me from lessons, to keep a weather-eye on the window, to worry not about the timetable but the tide-table. A prospect of the sea within sound of the sea, piers and jetties and harbours, boats inshore and ships on the skyline, tugs at me now as I write, like a mooring, hauling me back into the solitude and unlonely loneliness of those shoreline days. This was my self in the making.

By the time I was ten, about three years before we moved

to the wooded hill, when a different balance between the hill and the sea was struck, the coast took strong claim on my free time. It is hard to accept now what fishing there was to be had on Colwyn shore, between Penmaen and the point of Rhos when I was young. Nothing like it survives, just as nothing like the freedom to come and go remains today for children as young as we were. 'Drive carefully, free-range children at play', I saw on a sign remote in Argyll the other day. We were free-range children in every way, except as to word from the unknown world.

It was quite early one morning would be the way to start to tell you.

But it started well before morning. It was afternoon, is closer yet, if there's a beginning to find, the day before, in the backyard at 'Thornfield'. Eleven going on twelve, twelve going on thirteen, I'm a free being, too young to be employed in a holiday job. With all the time in the world on my hands, except the time of the tides that rule my thoughts, I'm away in my dream, trying my hand at a nightline.

My ambition is unlimited. I'm all imagining without a thought in my head of failure. Every hook I'm tying to the line on its little length of 12lb breaking-strain nylon will take a fish in the course of the night. You believe it. I bite through the nylon droppers at the knot, tough bite through tough line for young teeth. I'm so hooked I think of nothing but being ready for the night, as the afternoon softens in the yard and my mother calls me for tea.

This boy that I was – I remind you – is eleven going on twelve, at the youngest. The ages of eight, ten, thirteen are defining points of moment in his story and make it possible to relate it with some degree of accuracy, as to what happened when. He won't reach thirteen before his world is transformed and he's transported elsewhere, away, seven miles off, under the wooded hill. There nightlines will lengthen unimaginably, dreams deepen and fish multiply. What he's doing now in the Red Wood is merely preparatory. He thinks it is the real thing. And so it is, until he learns otherwise. And as you'll realise when you reach 'The Black Lake' he's begun to harden just a little now, and has a slightly clearer sense of purpose, resolve discovered in the mountains at the Black Lake.

Soon you'll see him emerge with his nightline over his shoulder. The line consists of a length of stout, domestic electrical wire, rescued from the tip at Fairmount, hung with hooks on 'droppers', and wound round three sticks. He's slung the silvery canned-fruit bait-tin along the handle of his spade. And off he sets, both hands full, his spade over his other shoulder. The can slides now and then and bangs against the step of the spade as he walks, then slides back onto his shoulder. He's like a one-man band. There's a way to go to the shore, though not far as the crow flies. But he's no crow and he has to round Pen-y-Bryn and make his way down Llawr Pentre, daring the dank shadows under the viaduct where the rats come out in the evening, to reach Beach Road and follow the stream to the sea.

It takes some determination, certainty beyond doubt, to go to so much trouble, at such an age. What does he have in his head? And he still has to dig his bait: at least a dozen lugworms for his dozen and a half hooks. He knows he must pitch his line as near the margin of low-tide as he can, to maximise the time it's under water. That will make his night longer, his night of disturbed sleep and watch-checking in the dark between submarine slumbers. He has an Ingersoll pocket-watch on a leather strap, like an old man before his time. It ticks as loud as a bomb on the chair by his bed.

He must come down as early as daybreak to inspect the line, to see it come to light, or be pipped at the post by the gulls. They'll swim round his surfacing tackle and hack at his catch with their blood-tipped beaks if they can't snatch it away from the hooks. He knows this from experience already. He's learning every step of the way lessons never to be had in school, things too that he doesn't know he's learning: resolution and independence and how to survive on Inis Mór, though as yet he's never heard of the place, on which his future's converging and his folly, at thinking to resist the world and its business.

So now it is dusk. The tide is slack at low ebb, right at its last of land and motion, and the night lies ahead, at Easter towards the last of spring, or at the front edge of summer to September, as school holidays run. Lamps are glowing dimly along the promenade, gaining strength as the sun lapses, all the way round to Rhos. There's no-one about but that boy and a few herring gulls, right at the tideline, a dog barking at gulls at the sea's edge and its owner strolling along the sand, below the point where Colwyn stream disperses into shingle and sand, far beyond the longest breakwater. The ribbed, the chevroned sand is soon mole-hilled where he's digging....

Evening stretches itself out in every direction, darkening quicker inland, thinning more slowly to silver and shadow at sea. The pier is stranded on its little legs, as if too cautious to go the extra few yards to dip its toes in the slack tide. Lights cluster at the landward pavilion, but the length of the pier itself is unlit, except from this angle for a green starboard light at the pierhead. A dank darkness gathers under it. Hove to off Penmaen a quarry-boat rides, minimally lit, waiting for the morning, when it will come in to the old wooden jetty at the easternmost margin of the long wide bay of Colwyn. This is not a shore to offer much of a port in a storm for a good many miles. Captains must look elsewhere whichever way the wind blows or stand off far out and ride it through.

The nightfishing boy makes a start. It's a daunting business at first. The sand has drained. But the lugworms in their underground hammocks, slung between dimple feeder hole and cast are thickest where it's wettest, not on the dry banks. The tide holds off. It hasn't turned. It won't turn for half an hour perhaps. But when it does it won't be backward in coming forward. He's digging as fast as he can. The spade must go down deep and fast and be turned smartly, or all he'll see is the worm's greeny sandful tail slipping away as the water wells in. Nor is this the first time he's dug for bait. You can tell he's served part of his apprenticeship at least, making ready to fish at the end of the pier. Not for him Darky Lee's 'fresh bait', sold to tourists from his shed on the front, down below the station. Not for him the packets of salted lug at the tackle shop.

But what solitude and solitary determination. The sand sucks and socks about his spade. In these wetter reaches the going's heavy, and the worms are quick off the mark. He'll chop one or two perforce, and stain his fingers yellow. But hook-length pieces will do, and then he'll start to take some whole, reddish worms, and here and there a big black one, of a length to make up for two or even three lesser mortals. The moment he turns one he darts in like a gull to pick it out. The gulls are already hovering and shrieking hungrily round the molehills and water-holes he's left behind him. Sometimes he has to hold onto a worm for a while and little by little ease it back from its urgent escape, trying his best not to let it break in two.

Soon he'll have to cut his losses. Some hooks will have half a worm, some a whole one. The tide has turned by the time he's driving his stakes into the sand with the back of his spade. His line's not straight but set across the tide in a 'V', arms open to it. It seemed like a very long line when he had it in the backyard, but now it's dwarfed by the wide shore. The sea is almost over his wellingtons as he baits the hooks. His bait tin swirls this way and that swimming on the flood, as he keeps it looped over his forearm. His spade, planted in what was clear sand, falls as the water undermines its footing. He mustn't lose it. He has one eye on his hooks and can, and one eye on where his spade was when he last saw it, and struggles to bait the last couple of hooks. He's in over his boot-tops and his jeans are wet well above the knee by the time he's done.

As he turns to leave the shore he realises the figure up there leaning on the rail is his father. Alarm shoots through him, and mars the occasion. It'll soon be dark, he realises. But no, whatever worry he's had, it's all right. He's greeted happily. It's all right, and they walk up together, pausing to look through the dim and darkening light to see the big trout that lives up the drain pipe, opposite the public lavatories. Is he there? Can you make him out? Look, there he is, his nose at least, beyond the end of the pipe. He's big. How big is he? A wonder no one's ever caught him but folk must have tried or he wouldn't be so wary.

That trout intrigued me, tempted me. The stream ran quite deep and dank there, below a stout wall of dressed stone, just up the road from the railway viaduct. The tail end of a steep municipal garden petered out there, below the Priory on Cefn Road. On the opposite bank a path bordered at its end by a clump of canes led over a flat, concrete, railed bridge to the road and shore. The stream was then channelled under the promenade to the beach through a big round tunnel. You could straddle your way up that tunnel to the shallow last reach of the stream. Or should you have nothing better to do you could ricochet pebbles and cobbles down it and make a great echoing watery racket.

At high tide on a wild day sea-water might be punched

up into the stream in its lowest reach. But here beside the road the water was pure of brine, however otherwise impure, and clear, except after sustained heavy rain. I didn't obsess about the big trout but now and then he swam in and out of my thoughts. And I would plot his downfall when he did so. It was no good leaving a line there overnight. Someone was bound to notice, and take it, or beat you to the fish. Not that it'd be safe to eat it anyway, living where it did. I grew up to know it mattered that what I caught and killed might be eaten, and this it was that kept the big trout safe, at least for now.

But I remember well the afternoon I did for it – as with my snare I did for the big buck rabbit on the railway embankment above the Irish Sea – with tough resolution and Black Lake know-how. I hooked it out on a *coch-y-bonddu* dangled and twitched on a piece of nylon tied to a bendy bit of bamboo cut from across the stream. How he splashed and lunged, and jigged in the air, the cane bent double to my fist. I took him home, as if officially to record my skilful success. We weighed him in at just under a pound. Then we put him in the dustbin. It would have been better to have left him to live out his days fattening on sewer-juice. But I'm answering the questions you won't ask, now, as frankly as I know, ready for when I'm gone, as to what my growing years were like, no punches as to barbed-hook barbarism pulled.

Once home in bed that night I didn't think of trout at all, but of whiting and flounder, codling and plaice. I loved to catch flatfish. I loved their queer look, with one eye round the corner, the other overhead. Their chins turned up, as if they were about to blub at their sorry flat-earth overhead horizon. Ever since the world rolled over, and they got out from under it by the skin of their teeth, there they were condemned to the bottom of the deep. Yet all their dreams looked up, from the wrinkled sea-floor, through a wrinkled roof, to stare at a wrinkled star. I loved their rusty stigmata, and I even quite liked eating them – the one fish I liked on the bone, because their skeleton made them so easy to tackle.

I lay there thinking of my line and took comfort in the quiet of the night. It was a still night. You could hear the owl across the Glen in the still trees. The sea wouldn't wreck my line, sag it with weed, uproot its stakes, half bury it in sand, still less wash it away. It was a perfect night, but not for sleep.

I live nowadays about as far from the coast as it is possible to live in the unnameable archipelago. I can't set a nightline anywhere but on a page. I can't lie in disturbed sleep impatient for the day, except when I have a line or two out towards a poem. Fish and poems: you dream them both into being and then they press against you, nose you awake. It's not quite the same. But it is similar, being linear and of the nature of possession. And it's also a matter of luck, notwithstanding craft and knowledge. And so there you lie, tucked up in bed fathoms away, if you can sleep, that is.... But your sleep at best is as turbulent and crossed by currents as the sea. Intermittently you keep the night watch, the dog watch. That dawn will come is the old argument from experience. But when?

Starting suddenly, as if hooked from my sleep, I'd find it hours away yet, and still so again, and so slow you'd think it at the bottom of the world and never to dawn. Then when I'd be at the bottom of the world myself, something terrible would prompt me to wake. The hour had come just when I wanted another ten minutes, another hour, just when I didn't want to stir, still less rise and shine. But there it was the hour of my doom and up I stole bleary-eyed to hurry unwashed into my clothes and run down to the shore before the morning was too many minutes older, the tide too many inches lower.

Here came the first train from England, trailing silvery-grey steam clouds, hauling the day with it, to station after station, impatient for Holyhead, rattling now over the viaduct as I ran under it. How far out was the sea? ...And there it was limping out, scarcely ruffled, slow to wake from its own night's nuzzling against the sea-wall. And there was I escorting it back, like Moses dividing the waters, restless for the first sight of my unpromised catch. And then when I saw the tops of my stakes, slightly askew now, how long before I could learn my luck or lack of it?

What a thrill when there I saw, not two, not three, but nine fish in a row, whiting and a ling. It was an intensely bright morning and I remember thinking the whiting at a distance looked like starched handkerchiefs pegged at a corner blowing on a washing line. That sort of a catch set me up for many days and nights of failure, of disaster, of lost tackle, and frustration, until success felt like the dimmest memory before round it would come again, to hook me.

Such an event it was too, one pristine morning at low tide, at the end of the pier, at nine o'clock, when, as I was fishing from the eastern corner into two or three feet of water, my rod bounced on the rail so hard I might have hooked a whale. I struck back. But missed the fish or whatever it was. So I must reel in to check my hooks and bait up again, as nimbly as I could, not to lose a moment, all the while concentrating on the angle and range at which my original cast had been. Out went the paternoster on a wing and a prayer and my reel whirred round to almost the last of my line. (I had a cheap rod – with a bamboo lower part, and a greenhart top. My reel was an old-fashioned wooden one. Not even a fully-grown man could have cast any distance with it.)

It was heartbreaking to think the monster had escaped.

Nor did I expect to connect with it or anything again. I was used to blank trips. But almost at once, bang went my rod on the rail again, so vigorously that its butt-end skidded and the rod slid sideways on the rail. This time the fish stayed on, and up I wound a plaice bigger than any dinner plate we had at home, a surfeit, still flexing and alive when I got it home and into the sink, to clean away its purse of gut and foreshortened alimentary system. Not only was it bigger than a dinner-plate, it went a good way to filling the bottom of the sink.

I've never caught a bigger plaice since, except later when helping aboard Mr Arundale's trawler, the *What-Ho!* - between Trwyn Du and Great Orme's Head, working Dutchman's Bank and Lavan Sands. It was so marvellous that rather than persist in the hope there might be others like it out there, I packed up my gear almost at once and hurried back home down the prom and up the Donkey Path shortcut to the village. I was so thrilled I couldn't wait to show my catch. I had other such days, each of a different order, and few perhaps, few enough to make them seem to have occurred many more times than they did.

★ ★ ★

Big fish and big catches are like big snows. A shoal of fish and a blizzard and a starry sky are one and the same in the mind's eye of a boy. It didn't snow every winter. I can't pretend it did, even in those far-off days; and rarely did snow stay long on the coast. The salty air and warmer air currents by the sea worked against it. Through the images of snow still falling silently in my memory, I can make out perhaps three starveling snowbound winters in my first twenty years.

Even so I'm blinded, wide-eyed flakes stinging my eyes,

and unsure of my direction, unsure how to tell one big snow
from another. I later wrote a poem about this business and
called it 'Sledging':

> Just as less can be more, rarely can be often.
> It's not so much the mind-body problem as
> the nature of truth and its conditions, the meaning
> of memory, the soul and its survival in the world,
> whirled in an infinite number of dimensions and planes.
>
> So I protest to myself, anyway, admitting
> when I say 'I used to', it might be I mean 'once'.
> Upon a time, below a time, events winnow out
> their chaff. So with the grain, against the grain,
> the song steps out into the blizzard of the page.

How rarely was there snow enough for sledging. I'm not
counting the big snow of '47 which I survived but could
hardly be said to have witnessed to remember. Forget that
memory starts its work before we're born.

But there was one Boxing Day, the one before I was
thirteen, in which snow and fish came magically together at
the end of the pier. Stars might have too, but the snow-
clouds obscured them. I made a poem about it that opens
with words of my great-grandfather McNeillie, and folds
into its account the much later experience of seeing *Dr
Zhivago*, a cold-war film of the greatest force and moment
for my later youth and its romance. But the snow in the
poem and 'The Whiting' of its title date from Red Wood
days on Colwyn Bay pier:

> Snow falls when you least expect it.
> A rural saying to amuse the sceptic.
> But none the less
> a clichéd Christmas greeting
> fooled the coast that year
> with stinging flakes, as perished flocks

of redwing refugees in comas
fell dying through the silent branches,
out of Scandinavia,
or a northern elsewhere, anyway,
its serrated horizon of pines
sawing the blue cold of a brief day,
as glimpsed at the Odeon
by Sharif's Zhivago.

That day we went to the pier-head
and fished all evening in a yellow storm.
And as if to show
how dreams-come-true
establish norms, the whiting rose
in blizzards from below
and stormed our hooks
at every single throw
until they skidded round our boots
in translucent lobes of ice
their eyes like melting snow.

So that was my seaboard Red Wood life. But I kept another
world too in those years, and other company than my own,
as you will learn.

THE BLACK LAKE

My birthday falls in August, on the glorious or not-so-glorious twelfth. So for a minor miracle I was still ten in May 1957 when I passed the eleven-plus. That was the watershed exam that divided children as sheep from goats. For me it was life's first stark lesson on the subject of equality, to say nothing of liberty and fraternity. And if I didn't see it in those terms, as I could hardly have done, not being any kind of genius, I nevertheless felt its barbarity. My best friend Dick went one way, I another. I was saved and he was lost. Our respective places in the scheme of things were decided for the rest of our lives. Little by little we grew apart. Not that I didn't know the stigma of failing an exam. Up until then I'd proved as good at failing as the next boy. As I am still, at falling short in life's hard way. But wonder of wonders, to me at least, I passed the eleven-plus when I was ten.

I don't remember the occasion for any noble reason, as to injustice, or out of pride. I remember it for the reward it brought me and the change in my life beyond school and the Red Wood road that it wrought.

My reward for passing was a three-piece Greenhart fly-fishing rod made by Alex Martin, bearing the name SCOTIA. This SCOTIA became my pride and joy, even if I never quite forgot that it wasn't a split-cane two-piece Hardy 'Perfection' such as my father had bought on our Irish adventure, at Watts Bros, No. 18 Inns Quay beside the Liffey (no longer in business), when I was a little short of five. I remember all that, as if it was yesterday. I carried Perfection through customs. This was in case it might catch the excise-man's eye as a new purchase and attract duty. So years later my father would smile to recollect, amused at his caution, amused at the way the world was then, just after the war.

SCOTIA means Scotland and for me that endowed my rod with superior qualities, even beyond perfection. SCOTIA's dark grainy wood pleased my eye. I seemed never to tire of inspecting its varnished surface, of assembling its three pieces, its delicate, springy top-piece, and taking it down. The silver rings to guide the line had their mounts whipped in place with black silk. This too shone under a coat of varnish. The ferrules were similarly bound, and there were little lugs of silver wire whipped in to serve as grips for your thumbs to help you dismantle the rod at the end of the day. Which could be a struggle, on a cold wet evening after a cold wet day, in a small boy's perished hands, away in the mountains, miles from home. The whole thing would catch the sunlight, if sunlight there was and the water dappled, blinding bright, in a brisk breeze. And it had a proper cork handle. It was the real thing and not a hand-me-down either, as almost everything else had been, apart from an airgun called *Diana*. (I brooded especially on an antiquated bicycle called 'Hercules' painted bright green for me one Christmas: most humbling the absence of shiny chrome; the once-rusty wheel rims painted black, the handlebars green. How other more fortunate boys looked down or askance at me and knew my status.)

What was most important was what SCOTIA set afoot. It was a magic wand. I practised wielding it, in the backyard at 'Thornfield'. I was just about to come of age, at all of ten years old, my heart greener than the greenhart tree, if far from innocent. No one can be conscious of being innocent, except of a crime. I'm sure I've never felt innocent. I knew guilt at heart, from the start. It tinged everything. How it got in I don't know. But I know what fuelled it was fear, a fear to be feared indeed, and temptation, not to do what I was expected to do but to escape it and go my own way.

With SCOTIA and its necessary accessories, happy cast-offs this time of my father's (reel and line and fly-box etc), arrived new boots, my black 'oilskin', my sou'wester, gear fit and unfit for the worst of wilderness weather. With it too, at last, came my deliverance from Sundays at home with my mother and sister. Goats from sheep, I entered the world of men and legend, a slip of a boy, hardly weighing five stone. From now on I would feed my own wide-eyed reservoir of dreams and future stories.

I had lived for this moment, longed for it consciously and no doubt subconsciously. I'd even wept for it in the small hours, hearing my father on the landing and the stair, as he tried not to make a noise, closing the back door, and making good his escape down the side of the house, into the dark murk of the bottle-green morning and away. To what? From what? What mystery at heart? Escaping to and escaping from being inextricably coupled motives and motifs. I would find it all out for myself in good time.

So, as you see, passing the eleven plus meant the world to me, but not for the usual reasons. It meant escape, escape from home. What if I'd failed? It doesn't bear thinking about. Would SCOTIA have been my consolation prize? I can't think so. But I didn't fail and now no longer did I have to endure the day, waiting for my father to come home. No more did I have to play shop with my sister in the little cupboard in the alcove, or some such nonsense. She knew my heart wasn't in it. She it was I once when quite a lot smaller rebuked as a 'blooded fool', meaning bloody fool, over some incident in that shop of hers. She it was who otherwise called me 'the witness', she of the village Band of Hope, if not the Jehovah's Witnesses.

What did I witness on the home front? Nothing special, as you know. Those ordinary goings on, family life, differences, squabbles, arguments, violent outbursts of rage.... My sister's line was that I didn't participate, didn't do my share, didn't keep my end up, didn't protest at parental injustice. It was hardly the thing in those days anyway. I kept my distance, later at least, I'm sure. And I saw the heart of melancholy itself, I believe, of longing for what I couldn't have, of inarticulate loss thereby, from the start.

But whatever my sister's view I used also to chatter-chatter-chatter, and I was called a jabberwocky. My father would thump the table angrily to shut me up as he tried to listen to the news on the wireless. Undaunted I would continue whispering loudly to complete what I wanted to say. So I was any number of things, at that age, just as I am now. Except then I longed to be a man and go fishing for trout at the Black Lake. Which none of you did, I think. Or I feel I would have met you.

I bore witness to the brown trout and the wilderness, in life and death, and grew quieter and more withdrawn, as if spell-bound. Whatever my earlier flights round the tower of Babel, I made up for them in silence soon enough. It wasn't so much that I held my tongue, or kept my counsel. I just grew more inward, a receptor, not exactly pensive. I think therefore I am should here read I think therefore I was. Beyond home, among my peers, this withdrawal became especially marked, but at home too, until I was never quite at home. If I'd known what a *cogito* is mine would have been: I don't think, therefore I am, lost in the depths of things.

Sometimes my father would exclaim aloud at the sadness

he saw in my look. He'd see me absent, and distracted, both when I was a boy and later, in first manhood. It pained him. But I think I was very happy in my melancholy, if now today no longer free from deeper sorrow. I was cast that way at birth. But man's inhumanity to man lends bias too. My father was a fine one to talk, anyway, in all the gloom that held him fast from day to day, so rarely lifting, so rarely light of heart, never it seemed at ease.

Now no more was it my sole compensation to gut and clean the fish he caught. This I had done in the high sink, under the cold tap, beginning when I was about eight. My brother was born when I was eight, and I did some sudden growing up, on being displaced, driven farther aside and farther into my self, a middle child now, and most fortunate in that, slipping from attention, pioneering no parental anxieties, inspiring no new cares, not needing nursing. How I loved my brother, and we all spoiled him: he was like a special gift. And I was doubly lucky he came along: for his arrival set me free; he served my solitude and independence and sharpened my sub-conscious focus.

I loved the work of gutting fish too, especially if the fish were big, though they were almost never more than three-quarters of a pound. Fish fascinated me. I loved them. I prized them. Every time I picked one up it was as if for the first time. Fish and fishing filled my head, made my head swim.

The characteristic Dulyn fish was dark-backed, as if dyed by the black water, sometimes with a golden underside – sometimes paler, depending much on the time of year – and strongly speckled with red. The Welsh word for trout is *brithyll*. One meaning of *brith* is speckled. The characteristic black peppering of speckles common to all trout was less clear to see on the Black Lake fish, especially above the lateral line. Often too the Black Lake *brithyll* was short and stocky. I believe a close Welsh equivalent of *brithyll* would be 'common speckled fish'. So acquainted with them did I become that I could tell from the common speckled fish my father brought home, whether he'd fished at the Black Lake or a different water. In time, like a wine taster pinning a vintage to a year, to a village or a vineyard, I might just tell you which different water, the fish being, like an accent, precise to their place of origin. Sometimes the Dulyn fish had pale pink flesh and then it was said they were especially toothsome.

How I would look forward to my father's return and the ritual gutting and cleaning in the half-light of Sunday evening, the water seeming to get colder and colder, as it splattered out of the tap, all the way from the lake properly called Caw Lwyd but known to us then as Cowlyd, or when we moved to the Wooded Hill, all the way from the Black Lake itself. Then I cleaned the fish in their native water.

The world came round for those fish and for me. And the world was Welsh, as only much later would I see. In time I learned to inspect their gizzards, to find what insect life the fish had been feeding on. It meant everything to me, to see the fish, to wonder at them and to rejoice, to ask my father how he had enticed the bigger ones to rise, with what fly. So insistent was I and persistent in wanting to share in his expeditions and be close to him in that way.

So much did I love the brown trout, but not to eat until later in life. I loved it even when the bright-eyed shine had gone from it and matt rigor mortis set in, supplanting slithery slippery-eel suppleness.

It seemed my father always caught fish, whether anyone else did or not, brown trout from the Black Lake, or once in a way another place, Caw Lwyd, or Llyn-y-Foel high up under Moel Siabod, or Llugwy, or.... Names of such weight and depth to me, I drowned in them, as I said them to myself, a Sunday litany, a catechism, of longing. Places I could smell in my father's clothes and gear, in the bits of moss and other vegetation that got bagged with the fish, wet outdoor scents mingled with oilskin, when he came home. It was an intoxication to take to bed and sleep on, on the too-short journey to tomorrow. School in the morning to fend from my mind.

My father in his day fished every such North Welsh water known to man and some unknown, and others metaphysically, that he never found all day, out on the wilder moors and mountainsides, where anecdotal accounts of how to get there proved unreliable and maps stubborn to read, landmarks elusive to mark, ways hard to find. There were more than sixty lakes in our world, the world of Eryri, or Snowdonia. I would fish only a handful of them. Having explored far and wide, my father found the Black Lake best of all, as a challenge, both to get to, deterring others, and to fish. He loved it as no other water on earth, unless it was the smithy burn at Malzie, of founding memory, where as a boy he hooked his first trout and was hooked in turn, forever. It was his devotion to the art taught me the nature of faith and meaning. Some things have to be believed to be seen. Some fish must be imagined to be caught. The proof of life is passionate and unswerving devotion to dreams. As Yeats said – another fly-fisherman too – that's where reality begins.

Of course there must have been blank days I overlook here, when all my father came home with was an empty creel, too tired to be gloomy at failure, and the day up there itself more than compensation.

★ ★ ★

Now with SCOTIA at the ready, I was of the company, a boy-man among men (Ifor and Trefor) as they were men among themselves, or my father's sole companion for the day. I loved it especially when we went on our own. We delayed more. There was no one else to consider. We fished Afon Dulyn, the little stream that ran from the lake, especially if the water was up and danced around the boulders, foaming, purring, pouring, into black pooling holes, on a bend, such an enthralling sound-warp there. Such an inscape was there instressed in that rollrock highroad burn. Then the morning rise at the lake might be sacrificed to my instruction in casting, to the purism of fishing a small fly upstream.

My father would not fish, but crouching behind me, he'd coach me, correcting my action, and delighting in me when fingerling trout haloed overhead on my line, lured by the Welsh *Coch-y-bonddu*, the ignoble Bloody Butcher, the noble Mallard and Claret…. or the little black fly he designed himself, the bottle-brush fly that floated dry along the sheer surface of the narrows and rolled and bobbed in the turbulence of the pool, upstream, in those sharp acid-rain waters. There the small trout rose with roses on their silver flanks, to initiate me and be returned, instinctively, tenderly by first nature, to the dashing stream.

Then it was the same on the way home. But now we fished downstream, across stream, and in the dying evening when more fish chose to feed, in the thinning light, the cold air rapidly descending. Sometimes I'd hook one just big enough to eat.

When night began to close on us, my father might decide to trek away up the hill, on a vertical, knowing that to hit the track speedily would in the end make the final leg of our journey easier, no matter present suffering. Doing that one evening we stumbled on a rain gauge, a copper bucket in a hole, marked up in inches and fractions of inches. It had scarcely a drop in it, that high summer. So my father looked at me, and the next thing I knew we were bounding down to the stream to fill it, and then to struggle back a quarter of a mile or so and drop it all but full to the brim in its hole.

I could always depend on my father for lessons in delinquency. When I was ten, he was forty. We were ever divided by thirty years, as my son is from me, the true span of a generation, but sometimes it seemed scarcely more than half an hour. (The gauge we discovered was tended by the shepherd, who one day, with a knowing look, told of the time he'd found it full.)

So began my captivity in the wilderness, to things wild and wet. So I lay awake one fateful June morning in 1957, at 5.00am, pretending to be asleep, listening out for my father, as if fearful he'd forget me. At last he came into the bedroom and shook my foot through the blanket and whispered 'Lad, lad...' at which I pretended to wake suddenly. The day had come, the day of days. The eleven-plus was a watershed. (This is all a story about watersheds literal, littoral, and other, till the end of time for me.)

Normally the first day would be at the start of the season, which ran from 1 March to 30 September. It would not be in the month of June or May or April, unless March proved especially bitter and locked the lake with ice. It would follow the close season, as early in spring as could be. Mine had been a ten-year close season. Even before I could stand on a stool and turn the cold tap on above the old sink, trout fishing surfaced in my life. The close season – close and dark, a snug wintry tunnel with autumn at the entrance and spring at its exit – drew everything in.

How I remember those wintry nights, with the wireless on, or with my father hammering the typewriter writing about fishing, as often as not, or else sitting at his bureau under the crane of an anglepoise lamp, tying pretty imitations of the natural fly or nymph or larva. Winter might roar and rock about the house and the trees in the Glen or up on the *allt* crash and run like a sea in storm and flurry in the chimney, but we were snug indoors, in a pool of lamplight, absorbed at this miniature, delicate work, as if at the eye of a storm, the still centre, the eye of the hook.

As to tying flies, my father was like an old biddy with knitting patterns in her head: knit one, pearl one, knit two together.... He didn't need recourse to patterns. All the patterns were in his head, and next in his hands, which were unusually big hands, unlikely hands for such delicate manoeuvres. Then there were adaptations and inventions, theories to put into practice, as to what a trout actually sees.

My father had books on the subject, classic books. Their appeal to me lay in their pretty illustrations of the numerous varieties of imitations they discussed, and the feathers they identified. These books also had other guidance, as to key flies to use month on month: Iron Blue Dun for March and April, when it is cold, for example, a small fly on a number 16 hook. But that was not the heart of my interest. My pleasure was more simply sensual. I'd draw my chair up and watch my father's every move. His hands were so big that for significant passages you couldn't see what he was doing. It was as if abracadabra he conjured the bright pretty flies into being.

About him on the opened bureau lid would be all the materials needed for whichever design he was intent on: Lilliputian tins and boxes, scissors, tweezers, little spring-loaded clamps for gripping and winding the silk thread, and other miniature gadgets, and reels of thread: black, olive being the shades most in use but all the colours of the rainbow to be had in one or other giant cigar box (probably supplied by a Ratcliffe boss); and bigger reels of narrow lurex ribbon: gold and silver, and red; and gold wire; and wool, and quills, and hackles in 'capes' from the breasts of poultry: pointed cock hackles and rounded hen hackles, black hackles and brown and ginger ones: hackles of every kind and shade, some dyed ones of bright green or orange; horse hair; deer hair; dark hair from the hare's ear; mole fur; water-vole fur; tinsel; wax; pheasant tails and tippets and wings; peacock herl and ostrich plumes; blackbird wings and tails, and song-thrush wings and tails; blue feathers from the wings of jays; starling hackles and wings; coot and moorhen feathers; heron feathers; teal, mallard, widgeon, partridge, grouse, woodcock, tawny owl feathers.... Every feather that ever took wing, it seemed.

Such an evening would smell of moth balls and nail polish and other potions, and it resounded with a jew's-harp ring, created as the little hooks, gripped tight in the vice, received their first whipping of silk along their length, from bend to eye. I loved that noise. I loved on those occasions especially the scent of nail varnish, a beadlet on the point of a needle of transparent nail varnish being ideal for sealing the last hitch round the neck of the fly, once the thread is finally cut.

I loved the way the cock hackles would spill into a whirr of insect legs when wound round the shank, just behind the eye of the hook. And all manner of other effects delighted me, as the different materials were applied and the imitations completed: sedge fly, stone fly, caddis, nymph, beetle, spider, daddy long-legs, May fly etc, etc. You could not have enough flies. And as each one was made and set down on the desk, the mind could not help leap to ponder the trout it would take, to reflect on the lake, to imagine spring. Just so I would summon the lake to mind sometimes, when my mother filled the kettle.

You needed a great store of flies. Few survived the mauling they got when a trout rose and took the hook. Many besides were snagged and lost in the back-cast, or had their barbs ripped off by rocks, or got waterlogged and lost their glory. Veterans of successful days battered beyond further use would be hooked into jacket lapel or hat. My father wore successful flies in his hat, until it was so festooned with them you could barely make out the hat itself, for the besieging swarm of insects that forever buzzed about his head.

So the close season, when no fishing was done, had both a practical and a metaphysical role to play. Fishing went on. Fish were caught in the mind's eye. By the age of twelve I was tying my own flies, and there was a pride in it that made you prefer only to use those you'd tied yourself. Anyone might catch a hungry trout on a worm, but on an imitation fly, and one you'd made yourself? That was the heart of it.

And in another part of the dark wood of those days and times, outside with my airgun *Diana .177* – goddess of hunting – I would go to shoot a blackbird or a thrush or some other innocent creature, and be rewarded with a sixpence or a shilling for a good pair of wings. And away my father would go shooting wildfowl and game and every kind of edible bird or creature for the pot, and in the process furnish an abundance of materials for the close season task of tying flies. Nature red in tooth and claw was first nature to me to know.

We didn't drive to pick up Ifor at his house on this first trip, nor did we ever, but waited parked in the dim first of morning outside Ratcliffe's. Ifor lived on Fairmount and would now be coming down the hill to Wellington Road, which Ratcliffe's factory faced. (I was born on Fairmount at St Andrews Nursing Home.) There was Ifor in his wellingtons on Wellington Road, it used to amuse me to think. He was the only one who endured the rigours of the day in wellingtons and he never seemed to suffer from blisters. His oilskin was black and heavy. It was a bigger version of mine. But he also had matching water-proof leggings, whereas mine were light blue and very stiff and I didn't really like them.

Nor did he travel light otherwise, but with a soldier's knapsack with webbing straps (just as my father had) and brass clasps, and his creel over his shoulder or stuffed in his bag, and his rod, his snack in his bag, his newspaper twist of black tea-leaves and sugar, his can and little bottle of milk, his matches, newspaper and tinder, or on some days in the warmer weather, just his *Thermos* flask and squashed cheese and ham sandwiches, to comfort him in the valley of the shadow of the Black Lake.

Ifor was an all-weather amphibious man. He had slightly bulging eyes, permanently surprised by the world, and wore his iron-grey hair slicked with *Brylcream* or *Brilliantine* back from his temple. His nose was round enough for him to look like a seal, or perhaps an otter, especially on a wet day. He was a kind of freshwater seal, a wet-fly man for all seasons and conditions, and an indefatigable, taciturn foot-soldier, who had been an infantryman in the war. Nothing deterred him and once at the lake he would fish and fish, casting and casting, the same three flies if he could, with rarely a rest all the day, but for a reluctant brew, and pause to check his barbs were intact, and not ripped off in the back-cast, among the rocks, a great hazard of the place and cause of lost fish:

> To fish there you wade in air among
> the rocks angling for your balance.
>
> Black water chops ashore and the torrent
> holds you bubble-rapt in its sound-warp
>
> like a dipper submerged in a rushing pool
> intent on caddis larvae.
>
> If one of the others came by to know
> your luck it could startle you to death.

Ghosts as they are, or not. They haunt here
like the stories they told of ones that got away.

The steep cwm will catch your cast more
than ever those wily fish might rise before you

to a hook ripped of its barb on a rock.
I learnt in this place, from the age of ten,

to curse like a man, 'God damn it to hell,'
to brew tea in a smoke of heather stalks and downfall,

to tie instant bloodknots and a noose
round the neck of the Bloody Butcher

while the fish moved out of range
as now that world has veered forever

and every finger's a thumb, my reading glasses
beaded with rain, and not a fish to be seen.

Ifor was a durable man, in the best way, as soft and gentle, shy and humorous, as you'd wish. He was palpably shy and would regularly blush, as if he was innocent. As if anyone was innocent. Don't we dwell in a fallen world? I assure you we do whatever your religious view or view of religion. But you always felt he was a man to be in a tight corner with, if ever you found a tight corner to be in. He had a stubborn streak. You felt you'd have to kill him to succeed against him. He caught fish. He knew how to do it. He had no fancy rod or reel, just old tried, trusted standbys of indeterminate vintage. He kept his own company mostly, as did we all, though sometimes if fate brought us in each other's way, the men might pause for a joint brew and a little metaphysics, about light and temperature and wind-direction and the feeding habits of the Black Lake's trout, a dour race, denizens of a dour place, about prospects, about likely fishing flies.

Solitaries we might be but we kept common worlds. We each had our trinity, our three lives: the one we escaped at home, work and school; the one we lived, here and now, in common things and the trance of thought; and last the dream-come-true by evening, weighed down with brown trout, none less than three-quarters of a pound in our creel, a full creel, never an empty creel, to cut into your shoulder for your trouble. We were nothing if we weren't dreamers, dreaming meaning into being.

'Diw,' Ifor winked at me, his lips pursed to smile, and chuckling to himself and to my father as he climbed in, 'I see you've brought the tea-boy, then...'.

Tea-boy I didn't take to. But the beauty of boyhood among men is that it has no voice, or hadn't one, in those days, when you were seen and not heard. Like a subject people, boyhood must be content to endure and bide its time. Boyhood dreams. It bears witness. It stares. It is capable of murderous brutality, with its airgun in the killing fields, its snares and hooks. (Or so it was all that time ago.) It is an eye. It is a soul and soul is never more fierce and beautiful than in its first encounters with the world.

Ifor and I had another thing in common. We had both passed the eleven-plus. That was one of the first things people would tell you about him, in some wonder. He had gone to the grammar school at Abergele. Would you believe that when you met him? The wives of the village would tell you, Ifor was a truant dreamer and a wastrel. There were those who claimed he wasn't all that bright. His eleven-year-old success must have been a mistake on the part of the examiners. Did they make the same mistake with me? (Don't ask.)

Sometimes at home things turned bad for Ifor now and then. Too many pints at the Sun, too many games of bowls or too much fishing. On these occasions he sometimes slept the night on a bench in the village hall. We seemed to know when he was in the dog-house and waited for him there. The prison-house of the grammar school had done little for him, perhaps, unless it inspired him to dream, as it surely did for me. You took him on to paint your house and one moment he was up the ladder and the next moment nowhere to be seen. It was as if the ladder gave him a leg-up away somewhere into the mountains (perhaps to Llyn Anafon, one of his other favourite haunts, haunted, as haunted me, by the story they used to tell of a fisherman who drowned there).

He knew the lakes at first hand, and he knew them from a classic book, a fisherman's Bible, that one day he'd give my father, *The Lakes of Wales* (1931) by Frank Ward. But he never talked to me about the book and nor did my father. I'd set eyes on it but I only discovered it to read after they were all dead, Trefor, Ifor, and John.

Who has not complained at not asking enough questions when young while the dead were living? The explanation is simple: we don't know what the questions are until too late. Here for whom I do not know, I am writing down my answers. So it goes round. And the truth is even harder, for hindsight's no more 20:20 than first sight.... Memory's selective, and writing must be more so, being founded in omission, where at best less might mean more.

We went to the Black Lake to fish and not to reflect on folklore and myth. The only myths we had time for concerned 6lb fantasy trout that no one ever caught. Though who never saw such a one, rising with a swirl like an oar's puddle? My father saw them all the time.

But here is what Ward's book had to say (his spellings preserved):

> "The Black Lake" is about half a mile in length and lies in a
> remarkable rock basin at the foot of the precipices of Craig-

y-Dulyn between Y Foel Fras and Carnedd L'ywelyn. Bare rock walls from 150 to 600 feet in height practically enclose it, descending steeply into the water. The outlet is very narrow, just wide enough for the small stream flowing from the lake, and the general aspect is decidedly sinister, suggesting a deep flooded crater. Dulyn may be reached in about three hours from Bedol Inn on the road from Trefriw to Tal-y-cafn. The trout here are shy but there are some good fish. Average weight is $1/_2$lb., with a chance of anything up to 1 lb. or more. The water is very deep (it has been sounded up to 189 feet), black and cold, and contains many rocks and stones. It is a late lake and fishes best at dawn and sundown in June, July and August, but owing to its remote situation, and the fatiguing walk to and fro, is not often visited by anglers. It is one of the impounding reservoirs belonging to the Llandudno Town Council. Permits are issued at a charge of 5s per day by the Waterworks Engineer, Town Hall, Llandudno. There is no boat available for anglers.

In the seventeenth century a belief prevailed that whoever, on one of the three "spirit nights" – All Hallows Eve, May Day Eve, and Midsummer Eve – watched beside this lake, would see who were to die in the coming year.[*] There were unfounded stories of deformed fish and of birds avoiding the lake, also there was a causeway running into it, of which the farthest stone was called the Red Altar. It was believed that in hot weather, to stand on the causeway and throw water on to the Red Altar would cause rain before nightfall.

This is what Ifor knew, along with whatever else he kept to himself.

(There was no charge levied to fish there in our time. 5s each a day would have been preventative.) Marie Trevelyan reveals that the lake was also said to be a point of entry into the Celtic underworld, Annwn or Annwfn, and tells that a dove appearing by those 'black and fateful waters'

> foretokened the descent of a beautiful but wicked woman's soul to torment.... Fiends would arise from the lake and drag

---

[*] *Folk-lore and Folk Stories of Wales*, by Marie Trevelyan.

those who had led evil lives into the black waters. Those who
had led good lives would be guided past the causeway
leading to the lake, and vanish in spirit forms robed in white.

It was for all of us an entry into the underworld of the heart
and mind, the soul itself, both when we were there, and
when we were not, the place we haunted to stave off the
world's demands and stresses on our time, the place that
haunted and possessed us. It was my first love affair. The
real thing, at first sight, and, in this case, at first hearing. For
I heard tell of it of course before ever I saw it, and I saw it
first in the mind's eye.

I knew only one Black Lake myth in those days and
believed it for fact, as did the others who told it me, and
who died before I could tell them the truth. We believed that
the aircraft flattened into the high crag, like a moth buckled
and splattered on a car windscreen, was a German bomber
that had lost its way returning from a raid on Liverpool.
Here was the war haunting my world again, like the
Laundry Hill siren, but no warning for those men and no all
clear above the mountain, just the ghosting mist and the
rock behind it. I used to wonder about the rear-gunner,
looking back into the night, as the plane concertina'd
exploding into the crag. Who was he? What were the last
seconds of his life? By what fraction did he outlive the
others in the cockpit?

You might still see wreckage up there now, for all I know.
It is some years since I was there (as in the poem above)
and I could see none then, the mist being down, tumbling
back into the cauldron. But it held great fascination for me
in those years and when we fished at the far corner below
the cliffs I would sometimes tire of catching nothing and
clamber up through the rocks and search among them,
among the bilberries, the myrtle and heathers, for bits of
aluminium, misshapen nuggets from the furnace of the

impact, or meccano-like strips of aluminium from fuselage, wing or tail.

Once I found a twisted piece, the size of my thumb, a slug of light alloy forged in the flames, from which protruded, miraculously, an intact light-bulb, something from the instrument panel, I suppose. I hoarded these little treasures in a cardboard fishing-reel box, for some years. But now when I'd like to cast my eye over them again, I find they have gone the way of all things, into the dark, into the underworld, where those airmen, or whatever burnt offering remained of them, fell to their doom.

They were Germans. They were the enemy and as a callous boy and youth I shed no tears for them or their nightmare fate. Hadn't 'The Dambusters' been one of the first few films I ever saw, in 'The Supreme', Old Colwyn, through a fug of cigarette smoke, the projection room like a gun-turret under fire, spluttering and flickering, and stuttering suddenly to a halt, as if hit, and the world gone black a worrying five minutes or more, while they spliced the celluloid back together or fixed a fuse somewhere, and we got into the smoke-filled air, airborne again, aboard one of those Lancaster bombers my grandfather had helped make, in an underground factory near Guiseley, banking up at the last minute on practice runs over the English lakes? Night-scenes, black lakes. Wasn't the war still the stuff of our comics and our lives? The Krauts, the Hun... our boyhood enemies, fought to the death in the Fairy Glen?

Now I know the true story: the plane was an American Douglas, not a German Heinkel, of the 27th Air Transport Group, bound on a flight from Le Bourget, Paris, to Burtonwood, on the morning of 12 November 1944. But Burtonwood was fog-bound and the flight was diverted to RAF Valley on Anglesey. It never arrived. Ten days later, tail overhanging the cliffs all that was recognizable of the plane, the scene of the crash was found, with mail scattered all around, blown here and there by the blast and then on the wind.

There died on the cold mountain: second lieutenants William C. Gough, pilot, and his co-pilot Richard Rolff; radio operator Corporal Hyman Livitski; and their flight engineer Staff Sergeant Kirk McLoren. RIP. What other memorial do they have than this? But that day in June I didn't know about them, though I knew about the plane, for my father had already brought bits of debris home, for me, and so began my macabre collection.

★ ★ ★

No one went into the mountains with greater fortitude and purpose than Ifor. Not even Moses. Not even my father who also never seemed to register physical discomfort, least of all in the name of brown trout. Though he once approved a retreat from just below eagle crag and the red rocks greatly to Ifor's disgust. I think he did it thinking of me, skinny-wiry wee man as I was, mindful of the time when I nearly caught my death of cold on a day of bitter unrelenting rain and had to be carried in to the house, running a temperature, feverish. At which my mother railed.

We'd not been at the Black Lake that day but fishing for salmon smolts in a little lake at the head of the Lledr, high up above Dolwyddelan. When we caught them we snipped off their adipose fins and put them back. It was a pioneer scheme to identify hatchery-bred salmon. I believe I was not yet ten but I'm not sure. We still lived on Red Wood Road then. But what I see clearly in my mind's eye is the old split-cane rod I used there, with its green bindings. And why would I have used it if I already had SCOTIA? I'm sure therefore this was an early expedition, predating Black Lake times by a year or more. We went there twice. The second time was a sunny day. I remember snatching a dragon-fly out of the air so as to be able to see up close what this beautiful thing was that I'd never seen before. And I remember that because I remember my father praising me for being fearless, not thinking such a vivid thing, as vivid as a wasp, might sting me.

Ifor's other passion was crown-green bowling. The first place vexed housewives would look to find him when he was truanting from painting their houses was on the bowling green. Though he bore no physical wound, like Laurence Sterne's character Uncle Toby he had seen action at the gates, something they said he'd been involved in, of men burnt alive in a tank. After which a man, windfall of war's storm, might be forgiven anything, and I wonder if it wasn't the trauma of battle detained Ifor's thoughts, and turned his head from house-painting, and led him to the bowling green, or into the mountains, the backside of the desert on a very different campaign. There was no out-of-battle counselling for his generation, any more than for those in Caesar's legions, or the tribe of Israel, or the heroes of Bannockburn.

When we became a foursome, after picking up Trefor down at Min-y-Don, a South Walean draftsman, he worked with my father at Ratcliffe's, and was a most melancholy and inexpert fly-fisherman, the first to put on a worm and sit forlornly with a fag and a brew. We would drive the empty road down the Conwy valley, past Bodnant road end to Tal-y-Cafn.

The river ran broad and tidal here, and stirring to the heart as waters are in the first of daylight. Herons fished there, and cormorants would ride the tide, and shelduck pattered about in the mud, and any number of scolding gulls harried in the quick flood of the morning. Rarely was there so much as a milk lorry or a bread van on the road, or a tractor, or a herd of dung-splattering cows crossing to or from early milking. So early would we be.

We crossed the river and wound up towards the hills, to Tal-y-Bont. This was the way – thirteen miles – my father used to cycle from the village, before he bought the 'brake', leaving his bike at Y Bedol (the horsehoe pub: lucky for some, on the way home). From there he'd set off up the steep and narrow, hairpin hill, past Tan-yr-Allt on the corner, and up another wooded hill – an *allt* a word like holt and meaning the same – the three-hour footslog to the Black Lake. Then all the way back he must come at the end of it. Were we physically harder then? We were, and what dreamers of the dream: that life is more than our betters ordain.

It was a talking point for my benefit on this first trip that I ran by Ifor in the Fairy Glen on the very day the eleven-plus results were announced and didn't stop to tell him I had passed. I still remember my surprise at being teased about this. I can still remember running past him. He had barely entered and I was almost out, running late for school. I didn't think it right to say.... It seemed like showing off. Nor did I know SCOTIA was in the offing. Nor did I know this day would dawn and that my apprenticeship in the art of fly-fishing was shortly to begin, and that I'd go to the Black Lake with my father and the other men for my initiation into the rituals of manhood come June. This was the beginning of the poem and its meaning, to sustain me against the abuses of the modern world, and so to resist them. As I do now as best I can and will to my dying day.

I could never hear the word *Dulyn* enough. And that was just as well because it had even begun to vie in my father's repertoire of hallowed places with *Clutag*, the farm in Galloway where he had spent crucial childhood and boyhood years. Dulyn, the black lake... Dulyn the mysterious, stubborn, unyielding and unforgiving black lake... the 'sinister' lake, where they said, untruly, no birds crossed; and where no one ever went and if anyone did, you knew he was the shepherd from Llanfairfechan, out with his jack-russell and mongrel terriers and folding four-ten shotgun, in pursuit of foxes among the rocks, to protect his flocks. Though once up there, one late summer afternoon, we met two elderly ladies in grey tweed suits, perspiring from their exertions, like sheep before shearing. They had come to see the lake. Refined Welsh ladies, students of myth, perhaps, ladies from Llangollen, maybe. Another time we met the engineer from the Water Board (there was a small pumping house tucked away under the slope beyond the overspill), the lake also serving as a reservoir as Ward says.

But I don't remember seeing another angler there and god knows what would have happened had we done so. The sky would have fallen. We might have stoned him to death or drowned him. So primitively territorial did we feel regarding that place. Though it wasn't really that we laid claim to it but that it possessed us.

***

You could only drive so far up in an ordinary vehicle, and how far depended on the time of year, in those days, in the fifties. Hard on winter's onset, the frost and snow would break up the bed of the track and shift boulders and create new potholes and perils. We used to stop way down after the first gate, above Rowlyn Isaf farm, a place that stood scarcely visible below the single-track road beyond a raised drystone wall. It was either a glorified *hafod* (a summer place) now, or a place on a Sunday where no one ever seemed to be about to be seen. Perhaps the occupants were huddled in the kitchen over their breakfast, or having a lie-in, on the day of rest, getting ready for chapel, or snoring off last night at the Bedol, oblivious of any sermon anywhere that morning.

What text would it have been? 'Now Moses kept the flock of Jethro... and he led the flock to the backside of the desert, and came to the mountain of God'? Or: 'I do set my bow in the cloud...'? ...Though now and then it's true I remember catching sight of a man there, disappearing round the corner of a building, the farmer or his son, or son-in-law, and once or twice a sheepdog barked, as we girded ourselves to be off, in the chill of dawn, as if we'd read Moses's tablets of stone. Then we would walk through the little wood, into which the road bowed.

The first stages in a walk of any ambition, any duration, out in the wilderness, seem always the same to me in this respect. They force you into yourself, your native self, to get the measure of it all, the reality of putting one foot in front of the other, the first steps of how many? The reality of the cold and unaccommodating air hits you. You must be your own upholder, within yourself. And how many steps before you have any rhythm and hope of making it to your destination? Steps that divest you of your daily life and deliver you into your body and out of mind, and into mind deeper than you know, deep as life itself. As if you are walking into yourself.

In this case it was also a matter of making it in time, in time for some passage if not the whole of the morning rise. The early bird catches the worm. Or in Trefor's version, the early worm catches the fish. O the crooked worm, the sinful serpent. Like members of some impossible religious sect, we wanted to be purists, to fish with the fly, and in my father's case a dry one – one that floats on the surface – given half a chance, and of his own designing. Poor Trefor was an apostate in our midst.

There were three trout rises in the day: morning, meaning first thing, not at that elusive fine-grained monochrome moment known as the *scraich* (blink and you miss it) but shortly in its wake. At some points in the season the morning rise lingered a little towards nine, sometimes beyond, on mild mornings. Then there were noon and evening. The first and last were the best, and if the first was always early, the noon rise was usually the most understated, the subtlest and the most elusive, some fish it seemed preferring to skip lunch or to sit under a rock with their sandwiches. Setting yourself to fish between the rises was more a matter of dedication and prayer than reason for hope. Though a rise might suddenly come on, stimulated by a hatch of insect life, and that is what we'd keep a weather-eye on as we toiled. There were seasons within the season too: March to early May, when the icy water began to warm and the fish were lean; late May and July, among the best days; August for dog days, not so marked up there (and when for two weeks we'd usually be elsewhere, on our holidays, on the Llŷn peninsula at Llanbedrog or away in Galloway); and soft and cooling September, for me always and still the best of them all, when the fish are ripe as fruit.

So keep up, run a step or two already, as the hare in the little wood, not a mountain hare, slender and blue, but an old bog-standard brown hare, delays you, as it sails zig-zag out of view among the regenerate bracken, in the shadows of silver birch, here and there stunted oak, rowan, thorn. This is a place of damp and moss, moss on boulders, on branches, and grey lichen, of sheep track, and low branches tagged with wool. That's not a blackbird flitting there but a ring-ouzel up from the stream. That's a wren, the king of all birds, and even there a robin, from the midden below at the farm. It's colder here at this time of day. The night has lain later here.

But run a step, your bag slapping your hip, wee boy, wee *bachall*, your breath visible on the cold air. Catch them up. The day is very young, younger than you are. Step up. They'll pay you no heed. They'll not wait for you or for your benefit. They have their minds on the time, on the light on the water away up there, miles of gasping miles ahead, where the kettle takes all but an hour to boil, especially if the heather's wet and the bleached waftage from the lake jammed in among the rocks, soggy.

Can you hear your father's voice as he anticipates the day with Trefor? They're speculating about a rippling breeze, so vital to fair casting and concealment, and a dimpling fish feeding at the point or in the little bay, or far round at the northwest corner where the stream feeds in off the cliff, from the windblown waterfall. They're thinking about trout and talking together about them, your father's voice the prevailing one. I can still hear it. (I'm sure it's close enough to call my own.) Fall in with Ifor if you can. He prefers more to march in silence a few steps behind the others. He'll look after you in his fashion. He won't see you as you see yourself. None of them does. But you're a boy soldier none the less, as if you lied about your age when they signed you up, to take the trout's shilling.

Then up on the brow now where the little quarry or cut would be the next place accessible for parking once the winter's new perils were mended. It's breath-taking now, literally, as the air is suddenly filled to bursting with buffets and tugs and the wilderness, north and south, opens before you, wide and barren, and the track narrows to a distant point away towards Llyn Eigiau. Here is our covenant, our bow in the clouds. Here's the poem of it:

> Air and cold light to take the breath
> from your lips, as if those looming clouds
> wanted moisture and the *llyn* didn't

mount and brim with melt and downpour
away up there at the head of the cwm,
March mad to be there as cold as winter.

They halted and parked up; jammed
a rock under a wheel, and set off.
The first stretch of potholed track across the bog
took ten gallon strides out of the boy,
and his oilskin chafed and the new boots.
But the Greenhart sweetheart *Scotia*

his rod and staff to hand, did comfort him,
before the full force of the wind
in the shock of his hair, at the red rocks,
and the distance was a dream to step into,
and none of it beyond his little strength
his stronger pliant heart determined.

When I wrote it I called this flawed effort 'Prelude'. Now I'd
call it 'Scotia'. But 'Prelude' was no careless allusion.
Though I was years from knowing it then at tender ten
years old, seven or eight years away from it, I suppose.
Discovering Wordsworth's epic was a revelation to me, not
just as to the territory of the Black Lake either, but as to
everything I lived, at the Wooded Hill with its winter
woodcock, and everywhere I went, and every dream I
dreamt, along the shore.

It could have been a poem about my childhood, a poem
about me. It gave me a shock of pleasure to find that poem
when I found it such as few things discovered at school ever
did, except Charles Baudelaire and the history master's
daughter. I didn't realise it at the time, but life in the
'unknown world' would shortly prove it, I *lived* a poem as I
grew up, between the Red Wood and the Wooded Hill and
at the apex of our days, stood the Black Lake, and in their
district I circled more besides, *ar lan y mor* down on the
estuary (wild with all regret, now), where no longer do the

bass press in like sex on the adolescent tide, as it chokes the river back upstream.

★ ★ ★

A ten-year-old perspective is barely sustainable even if it could ever be convincingly achieved by any other than a ten year old. Then how much of it could you take? Not much, not for long. Otherwise, who's to know it's not a nine-year-old or an eleven-year-old one, or just fiction, a gesture in the direction of the beginning, from, in my case, the vantage and disadvantage point of sixty years. Just let me try to hold my pen to the idea of it, and to hold you to it, on your first trip to Dulyn now, as if in the month of June, in 1957, whether you've been back since or not. Fifty years divides the truth of it (to the very month of June as I write) and adds it up again, making what?

Nor is it as easy as it might have been. It would be easier if that first trip had been the only one, the one and only time of vivid sensation in that place: once not often. Once and never again. I would remember it starkly. As I did when I went to that other black pool of water, Dublin – the same word with Dulyn – when I was four. The fact that no sooner had I been to the Black Lake for the first time than I was back again a week later, complicates the matter, and compounds it with superimpositions, like a negative multiply exposed. The single experience in a series is lost to the gaze and to remembrance.

The future reveals the unoriginality of all we attempt and all our vanity. It exposes the wiring invisible now on which we're strung. It is the granary floor. It is the ground on which we're winnowed. There's no originality but survives that process, and we don't know what it is or might be, from our perspective here and now, for every age has its take on such matters, and its own take on beauty, its vogues. But originality there is and truth will ring out and ring true forever. As only a base fool and empty relativist smart alec would deny.

Embarking on this writing, from the ground of my being, I saw clearly at once that the Black Lake should hang at the centre of the triptych. (Though I'm writing it first of the three.) I see it as the middle passage, a rite of passage, the zone of imagination and innermost being, the water-zone of wilderness and wet. My mind's I and my mind's eye. It is the trig-point at the apex of a telling triangulation. Telling being the word. (Tell me the story of your life, my father used to bid me, laughing, as we waited for the kettle to boil, huddled away up there among the rocks. Give me the benefit of your crack.)

But even otherwise the Black Lake occupies a border place, being the region that spills into the Red Wood and the Wooded Hill, whether by cloudburst over them, precipitated by the mountains, or by pipeline, into them, into your quickfire morning's groaning and wheezing kettle on its orange-and-blue bleary blurting gas flame and your first comforting cuppa, into that huge percentage of you that is water and water alone. At what point might you be water from Caw Lwyd, or water from the Black Lake, discernibly to forensic science? I have been both. Though now I am neither, except in mind, and that is more than enough.

As we go and pause for breath, or to enjoy the view, or both, I'll fill in any flashbacks I might have, as for example up at Clogwyn in knifing rain by 7am. I'll try to be as seamless as water, flowing this way and that, through time and truth. My witnesses on that day and all those days up there are dead. I could lead you a merry dance up the airy mountain and down the rushy glen, to my heart's delight if not to yours, and you'd be none the wiser, for there's no one to gainsay me.

But I won't. And wouldn't you be the wiser? I have too much respect for you to doubt it. The farthest cry though it be from your own experience, it wouldn't be the first time you spotted a falsehood at a thousand yards, or where have you lived in the unknown world all your life and what have you been up to?

★ ★ ★

Now it is serious. Now you know you have scarcely begun and the world seems huge, and there is some kind of fear in it, as you step manfully on behind the men, hurrying next to pass them, because you want to open the gate. But can you lift it up on its hinges and draw the ice-cold bolt at dawn? At the iron five-bar on the mountain road they'll take an early breather, to consume the long view home, the foreshortened view up ahead. It's still no nearer now, or easier, than when in those days they'd pause, to speculate about the weather and the rise, while I'd sail by to scoot the gate shut, swinging it to, with a clang that still jars through me, and as I grew older and with my youthful strength, kicked my heels to be off.

Now here I am like them, at the gate again with you, pausing with my pen, remembering how the year my feet grew big enough to wear my father's cast-off boots, I took giant manful steps ahead, hobnailed, to hell with waiting, perfecting the gait that still marks me out on life's road?

How I love a mountain road, its disappearing line, as if headed for eternity. The image of this one has haunted me ever since I used to walk it all but every week from chilly March to cool September. Though headstrong I am no more, if ever I really was. My head's weakened by the world's tragedy these days and I write from a consciousness of my own weakness, and loss. The already-fallen world lost, like paradise before it. What is there to lose next? Sense perception... the beloved. So make good your losses while you can.

I made that gate sing out on the mountain road, and went scooting in an arc round its tether, at first light, hinged to life. Now as I say I'm unhinged by remembrance and wrecked by grief at the horror, the horror of man's inhumanity towards the world, the devastated globe. But was it the first day I did that first? It's a long road and it has no turning right or left, until you're at its very end, where the spine of broken green floods out into boggy ruts grazed by sheep, or in those days it did, to more-or-less a sheep-path way, down to Llyn Eigiau, a shallow, silty, shrinking water under Craig Eigiau, not up at the head of its cwm. You can just make out from here the long retaining wall with the gap punched through it, the gravity dam that so gravely gave way and sent the billowing lake hurling all before it, down into Dolgarrog village, one tragic night of disaster in 1925. (*The Deluge* my father had called it in a tale he published in 1951.)

But the road was a rough track, and potholed, and broken, and if you ventured down it in the brake, you'd ground your sump, crack your – what was it? – your differential, wreck your exhaust. Now you can drive with ease to the parking place and join the centipede army of mountain boots, enemy of heather and myrtle, of moss and peat and stone and all wild life and nesting birds such as the heart has known.

Make no concessions? Take your stand against the heartless progress? Maintain it forever? It will be to no avail, drones the wind-turbine, and burns the laser-sun. Rome fiddles while we burn. But the stones know better and have the patience of Job, such as modern western man has not, in any measure, and what if he had, with his time running out? When the last home in China exchanges its old refrigerator for a new one, the balance will be tipped, the ozone game will be up, in the Oh! zone of a grief too late. Or will all this prove to have been a rhetoric of crisis as the West loses its way and Rome begins to retreat from its frontiers and to topple again?

But global disaster's what I hear, preacher man. What matter if the light comes on when there's no one left to open the fridge door? When there's no one to read the poem? Let alone write a new one. When the game is up, when all games are up, for poet and scholar, common humanity, honest poverty....? For who can tell a man what will be after him under the sun? Almost anyone, now: ruined settlement, roofless hafods of our time, decline and fall re-run, aeons before the game begins again, in the mists of time.

★ ★ ★

By the time he reaches what we called Eigiau Corner, a boy of ten has taken many steps from the farm back there; and must be up to as many and, being tired, more again at the back end of the day, all the heartbreaking way back from this next, old, rusty gate that you cannot ride shut, or open, but must struggle to lift on its hinges and buck over boulders and rough grass and rushes, or otherwise climb.

Now you are climbing a little and the roadbed is like a streambed, and running on the wind along it and rocking on both sides, as far as a boy of ten can see, a sea of heather and bog and rock and rushes, and copper and gold coils of dead mountain grasses, and the wind blustering through it, flinging up a skylark, a meadow-pipit in search of a cuckoo, a blue wheatear. Early in the season the dead heather there in grey March light had the look of a bed of kelp seen at low water. When it's raining steady cold rain and the mist is rolling off Eigiau crag you feel as if you are under the sea, down there on that stretch of track over the bog.

There's yet another gate, the penultimate gate, and the ultimate one might be open. This one is firmly shut. The rocks in my memory mount up more here, the track is almost lost among rocks, and then beyond the gate it zig-zags, between two lumps of outcrop, heather and gorse in their clefts, and a mountain ash. There's a bit of an old sheepfold here. There's a little-used fork just discernible to the right, below the ridge and round its base, leading to the dam on Afon Dulyn, east of Hafod-y-Garreg and Hafod Fach, ruins that speak of other lost worlds. Come this way I say to myself as I write, and disappear, never to be heard of again.

But to the left the way we're going, the track winds round and climbs along the length of the crag above, a terrace rising steeply. Here we might not stop before we reach the first brow. We'll pass the standing stone, a sometime gate post I think, with a blind cyclopean eye, and ear-holes right through it, and either climb the steep short-cut or go round the long elbow up to meet the new brunt of weather, a new seriousness, a new distance from the world below, a new isolation, and renewal of our covenant.

I never forget how this point in the way – this threshold – seemed to fill me with renewed resolve.

It was not quite this far up that we once cowered, in torrential rain, driving sheep out from their shelter, to take shelter ourselves like animals under the overhung hag, from the knifing rain and the wind behind it, wet through just about, for all our defences; and cold, and the weather on ahead lowering and livid. Then, feet turned to clay, the men agreed to beat the retreat and we turned back, all that way out, and all that way back. It was a ruined day, home by mid-morning and wondering, as I wonder yet, why did we not go on? 'He that observeth the wind,' goes the lesson, 'shall not sow; and he that regardeth the clouds shall not reap.' I adapted it this way in 'Glyn Dŵr Sonnets':

> That morning we got in under the hag
> overhang below Clogwyn, a sheep-shelter
> tagged with wool, and took stock, huddled there,
> as the rain drove home its attack, over bog
> and rock and wilderness of Wales below,
> the day still young and we already
> miles on our way, a raggle-taggle army
> of foot, with more than the worst to go.
>
> Owain, Maredudd, the old man, and me:
> a mere boy in their company, voiceless;
> on that cold, wet, mean March march to try
> our luck up there (with a March Brown?),
> but even they got cold feet (god bless!)
> and began to weigh up the march down.

Too much marching? Not this day though, not this day of days. Now we're up on the level of the bluff, Cerrig Cochion – the red rocks – on our right; Clogwyn yr eryr – eagle crag – on our left. Here the track is puddled earlier in the year and the puddles full of frogspawn. Here you gain your first view, if you only knew it, of the black cliffs of Dulyn, away beyond, at the very head of the *cwm*, 1,747 ft above sea-level, between Y Foel Fras and Y Foel Grach. But the Black Lake itself is not to be seen, and not to be seen until you are all but upon it, unless you climb high on the crag above Eigiau and the day's clear.

You are eager, your appetite whetted now. But I'll keep you waiting. You must learn patience on the lonely mountain. You must remember Job and his comforters. You must learn to wait and to watch the vacant day as it closes round you and becomes you, in your ten-year-old's dream. Until you are inside this place, and it is inside you, and nowhere else, and your mind is empty of all but what becomes your senses. This way you will come to see what's otherwise not there. As year succeeds year, this way you will find faith in things alone. I had an eye? An eye had me.

You'll mark where the sandpiper rose, above the stream, and where it landed, and work out where its nest is likeliest to be, and find it, and find the wheatear with her clutch in a hidden cup of grasses, under a lip of stone, and the meadow-pipit with the cuckoo's egg under her doomed breast, her rapid heart, in a little clump undistinguishable from any other little clump; and you'll know there's a trout quietly feeding, feeding invisibly, in that plunging pool, beside the boulder where the dipper dips himself dry, after diving for caddis larvae. You'll divine it as at the wrist of your being. You'll become a naturalist without study, by nature, first nature, second nature. I had an eye? I was an eye without a voice. Nature is rude and incomprehensible, at first, said Whitman, but don't be discouraged: it holds divinity enveloped in it. Divine it. It holds you, and you only knew it, bare-forked as a divining rod as you step into the religion of landscape.

Here at the ultimate gate we face our freedom, like the freedom of the open road. That old lie that we were everywhere born free will awe your ten years here before the mountain backdrop.

Now, if you wait here long enough you'll see four figures at a loose distance from each other, way down below in the valley, hot and bothered, following the stream in July. They've come from Rowlyn-isaf where they parked this morning. They thought to economise on effort and to reach the lake sooner than you and I. But look at them. They are already hammered, having joined the stream at Rowlyn-uchaf. They've fished the low pool at the little dam. They've fished, or one of them has fished, the lower reaches. There's no dissent in the ranks. But all recognize, coming up from

the trees, struggling to keep to the path of the stream, that
a mad decision was made. Someone had blundered.

I was one of those you can see, the boy, the one delaying
to fish, hurrying on to fish. Let me assure you, it was a day
of endurance almost as bad as any I ever knew, boy or
youth, and I knew some bad ones by then, if many far worse
days since. But I loved to fish the stream. It was more
manageable in scale than the Black Lake for me, and more
immediately varied in feature. You could read it. You could
hunt it. Except for the odd stretch or reach, it was nowhere
bland. So I didn't mind the slog and the staggering over
rocks and in and out of bog-holes, on and on and on for
more than half the morning, a close morning too, that July,
nagged and buzzed by flies.

★ ★ ★

Now, on this first day, just as we didn't follow the stream
from below Rowlyn-isaf, we won't cross the yawning valley
as logic might cry out that we do, but keep to the old quarry
track. A few steps on beyond the gate in a shallow puddle,
you'll find a ten-shilling note. Who lost it? When? Yesterday?
This morning? The men made much of it and gave it to me.
It would become a little talking point through time, holding
that wet blustery morning forever in my mind. But who
made the track and why? Who laboured to build the walls,
those at the lake that scramble up little short of vertical,
demarcating what? Keeping what from what? For whom?
Who whom? Who were those men who laboured up here,
for what reward, but the reward of being, in the wilderness,
speaking together in Welsh, singing Welsh things, belonging,
however exploited?

In a commonplace as old as the hills, it is often said
writing is like walking. The two are joined at the hip. It was

said of Henry David Thoreau, whose 'Black Lake' was 'Walden Pond', that he could write nothing if he kept indoors. Anyway, pen-in-hand, I've paused here at the gate longer than you know, a little oppressed by the next leg of the journey. It was a way we quite soon abandoned, for the shorter diagonal cut across the valley, down and up, and so much quicker, you'd wonder why anyone ever went off up the track, the incline steepish at first then gradual, the way long towards Melynllyn, the Yellow Lake: yellow, shallow, yellow with light, as Dulyn is black, and lively with fish at evening. Here on the way home we'd sometimes pause to fish the evening rise, after the Black Lake had proved unyielding, or to pick bilberries, and be plagued by midges, or both. The way back – let's consider it now – was hard and longer after a blank day. I would in my first years trail behind the men from weariness and have to make up ground.

It was on such evenings, maybe as we came fishless from Melynllyn too, the men might air the idea of trying our luck elsewhere next Sunday. I always liked the idea of elsewhere, and I'd speak up in favour. But they paid no heed to that. I had no say in anything at all. No more than I do now, except as to what goes on here, on this obscure page. And what say is that exactly? (Nothing you can do to alter. Think what you like.) But I loved the views of other ranges and the idea of other lakes beyond them. I could only believe luck might be better there. But then they'd talk themselves out of it, or during the week reverse their decision to go to Caw Lwyd, Llyn Conwy, or Llyn-y-Foel.

So conservative were they I can only remember going to any of these other lakes two or at most three times each, out of how many possible Sundays in any given season, down all those years? It wasn't that they were creatures of habit but they'd found and kept their vocation. As befits a novice, I wavered in mine. I especially liked it up at Llyn-y-Foel with its punishing climb up into the shadow of Moel Siabod. You must remember we didn't regard ourselves as mountaineers or hikers: we were fishermen and we wanted to fish not to climb, to conquer peaks or to sight-see. Our sightseeing was of the best, being blindly undertaken and incidental to a greater purpose. I'm sure that's true of the mountaineer too. Absorption in purpose soaks up most. I don't think, therefore I am.

Llyn-y-Foel is as light and airy a water as the Black Lake is dour and dark and easier to fish because easier to negotiate. What's more I caught fish there before I did at the Black Lake, lankier, lighter, more silvery trout than those at Dulyn, and how they lightened my heart and turned my head. But as I said we rarely strayed. We soon came back to the true quest and test and trial, our vocation and our deepest love and love-hate. Where you have still to find your way, to see the light.

But let me first take you the diagonal way to all but to the lake, before we resume, so that you'll know it, and make up your own mind when you come this way next. I mean to fill that world for you before we arrive, taking the three approaches we attempted in our time. There are of course still others, from over the top: but that day in my later youth, when I came over from Aber in a mist and along Anafon shore, I never found the Black Lake but found myself footsore at last in Bethesda, as if in the Bible, though not at any pool, or sheep gate, with no paralysed man, or Christ to cure me of my weariness. Bethesda, Bethel, Nebo.... So many Biblical names in that country of my birth, out in the wilderness.

It seemed momentous the morning we took the plunge, across the valley. I suppose that was only because I was so young. It's all because I was so young. Just as now it's because I'm not. I remember my trepidation, a sense of risk, as the old man set the angle of our attack. How the ground plunged and sprang and ran with water in deep clefts, heard before seen, in the thick grasses and mosses, the small occasional heather, of the long slope below Clogwyn Maldy that wanted you to descend quicker and more immediately than you meant to, so that you had to keep correcting your way, among the outcrop rocks, the flashes of bogland, the exhausting one-leg-shorter-than-the-other tilted terrain. Here sometimes we'd see a herd of mountain ponies grazing up ahead. Here one morning we found the skull of one in the bog and then all its skeleton scattered, dispersing. When we came back we brought the skull and jawbone home with us, a trophy in the stone 'potting shed', grinning pale horse of death, under the Wooded Hill.

On such an evening, making our way to the red rocks, we'd notice what a fastness those red-tinged rocks were, like a ruined fort, and because red (with iron), they looked as if the sun was setting on them even when there was no sun visible to set. They looked like something in an Arabian waste, a high place from which to way-lay infidel travellers. But we were of the true faith. We passed in safety protected by the trout-god, high in his mountain kingdom.

But onward and downward now, there was the head of the cwm to aim for, and the little rectangle of firs, of larches beyond Afon Dulyn, to keep in mind, to steer by. These trees had been planted it was said as an experiment to see how they'd fare at such an altitude, in such a place, to prove some or other theory about an ancient Cambrian forest. The better your angle of descent the more reasonable your ascent from the stream would be, in the last haul through the high moraine, the massive scattering of glacial rocks, some as big as houses, my father liked to say. And where to hit the stream but where it is easiest to cross, by the sheepfold, as it spreads out and becomes shallower and slower among the littered remains of the moraine. Here there was a slippery plank to cross by, like something in the Himalayas bridging a torrent, and we walked it, wobbled it, if the stream was high, with some sure risk of slipping off, on a wet and blowy day.

Now you are eager for the close. But it is chest-rasping this last haul up through the winding way, deeper and deeper into the boulders, towards the lake, in its looming gloomy black cauldron. You might want to halt awhile, half way, and take a breather. But the men won't. They're like a horse that has wind of home. It's all they can do not to break into a canter. They can scent lake-water in the surging air.

* * *

But now, rewind please. Don't think you've escaped to cast a line before us. Back up here on the cart-track we are already at the abandoned quarry near the Yellow Lake, where it rides full of light, under the summit of Foel Grach. Connected in some way to the abandoned workings, there was a small stone building by a stream. We called it the mill-house, and I believe it once milled stone, 'hone' stone – strange white soft stone on which you could sharpen your knife or the point of a hook. 'Melynllyn Hone Quarry' the map says. I never understood then quite what workings there had been. The map says many things. Settlement and Settlement in the most desolate spots. Whose Settlement? And when? Are these places where the Druids dwelt, ready to perform their lakeshore rituals, in the territory between the areas called Caerhun and Dolgarrog?

Way below us, water from Melynllyn spurted out through a broad-bore pipe, and down a splashway into Dulyn, and down the steep last climb to the lake, which we could now see, we'd step over miniature sleepers, and between old narrow-gauge rails, in places where these had not yet decayed entirely, rusted or rotted away. Quite close underfoot here and there you could hear the water gushing down between the lakes, through great cast-iron pipes. Now and then part of the pipeline might just break the surface.

What was that labour and what were the lives it commanded? What days? What talk? What stories? What pay? What nights and where were they spent? After a day's work what time to get home, what time to return in the morning? What Wales and whose? None of it on record, and oral memory of this place lost to mind?

How many steps have I taken now, how many more than the men, I can hardly bear to think, and every obstacle of rock or boulder, so much more to me to negotiate than to them. Next, it is a dizzy descent, taken at a slow steep step, and, approaching from the south as you are, by now you've glimpsed a corner of black water. And what time is it? And is there a breeze enough in that great cauldron, and are the fish on the move?

★ ★ ★

So this was it. This was Dulyn. This was the Black Lake.

Before me stood a rocky bay, the inky water in it joppling in the wind. So black it seemed unreal, this narrow south-east bay that runs up to the dam and overspill, with a small island of rocks in it. Round along the shore to the left were the remains of a boathouse of sorts, its corrugated iron roof all but rusted away, its timbers broken and caved, and no boat anywhere. I always wished it housed a boat still. There was said to be a boat across the little bay, in the little pump house under the slope opposite. The shepherd used to talk about it. But I never saw it. What a thing to steal it.... The idea of rowing out on the black waters in a small boat excited my imagination, and unnerved me too.

How I wished there was a boat to complete the picture, to swell the adventure of setting out. How much better the fishing would be, drifting towards those little bays, and along otherwise inaccessible shores. How scary it would be too, with a kind of vertigo to dizzy you, the lake being so deep, the black crag looming so high overhead. And when there were clouds blowing you'd not know were they moving or was it the crag. Who knows but you might feel compelled to slip overboard, into purgatory, just as up there on the crag you might be overcome by an urge to hurl yourself over the edge.

Behind me rose the steep way we'd descended and the gush of water from the Yellow Lake as it came slattering out of the pipe, to swell the Black Lake, provided a constant backwash to the immediate sound-scape. Farther to my left a few yards away rose a high crag and cliff and walls of stone and a lower terrace that stepped down to the water, steeply into the lake, forming a little bay within the larger bay, and a precipitous point of rock at which you could not round the lake on foot.

Underfoot were rough grasses and rocks and stones, in-between big boulders. Then all about a cacophony of lesser sounds and great, the enveloping sound-warp of the place. But though the place enveloped you in this way, its unrelievedness was so overwhelming it held you at bay in yourself too. It shut you out. It shut you in. It took you a while to acclimatize, always, to find the balance between inner and outer that is the dream-state where the world's your own.

After the exertion, you cooled down physically. Only on a rare summer day might you still feel warm after halting there a minute or two. I learnt the meaning of cold up there in my young bones. I learnt to get used to it and to endure, endure the cold rain, rain that might fall all day, with only a rare break if any. And rain at that height in the mountains is as cold and hard as granite. No concessions were made for me. None was possible, however many years I carried on my head.

What had I expected? I had heard so much about the Black Lake but I didn't hear anything like this. I had only known that it was, what? I hadn't known anything at all. It was a name merely, a word that in English was two words. I was a small boy. It was my father coming home with fish. It was the mountains and it was arduous to be there. But now this was what it was. The day began here, the quick day in the slow year of boyhood.

We set to, the men eager to begin and to disperse, my father greedy to drop a cast on virgin water, down in the little bay, out to the nearby point, round which you could bend a cast a yard or so, if the wind blew in the right direction and you were skilful. It was a spot where trout might be taken. (Where I once had two on at the same time, and lost both as Ifor tried to help me swing them ashore.)

My father had no after-you manners, no etiquette but first-come-first-served, as long as he was first. The others knew it in him. They knew their man and took no heed. So they waited for him at the end of a long weary day when he refused to admit defeat, last to leave last served, and he would cast and cast and cast into the evening, intent on showing us how to rise a fish. When by now all our thoughts were of home. As often as not he'd succeed, as if by sheer will-power but it was a combination of uncanniness and skill.

Up until then I had never cast a fly in earnest, except, up at the source of the Lledr. But I was thoroughly drilled in setting up and what flies to try, and so I too set to, the tea-boy still ten years old.

Like anti-social herons, the men went their separate ways. I'd follow my father all day. I had to be sure to keep in view or, sometimes, in sudden panic, he'd rant at me, so dangerous was the lake, so deep and cold and perilous the steep tumbled shore of glacial boulders. If you fell in your chances of getting out alive were slim to non-existent, slimmer than anyone ever said. My father, may I remind you, had a fiercely hot temper, as hot as molten larva, so I made sure not to drop from sight, if I could. He might fall from sight himself before I could realise it, before I could catch up. But the fault would be mine.

He could explode at the drop of a hat. So once at least I spent most of a very wet day in Coventry for leaving my hat behind. Though come early evening and the rain eased away, so did his mood, as if it had never been, and he'd joke about my being a dreamer, though my day had been a nightmare until then, the rain feeling my collar first, then seeping in, down my back and round my chest, to my waist, and my head plastered as if with Ifor's *Brylcream*.

I first cast my line where the stream from the Melynllyn pipe made a stir and did my best in the widdershins whirl of the winds. So this was it, and here the day began, an enormous day. It was a shock for me, I'll tell you, if you can have a shock on a slow fuse, a gradual, cumulative shock, an incremental shock in the accumulation of minutes into hours, a shock in slow-motion: hour one.... the beginning, again, to which the thread is made of filament, 3lb breaking strain (3lb to be optimistic), and you must feed it in that chop and bluster of the wind out through the eyes of the rod and tie your flies to the droppers and the end of the cast. Though I knew already all the knots to know and I doubt you do, the double blood-knot most testing of all, and could tie it blindfold, and in the highest wind, my back to the wind, like Trefor there lighting a fag in the cup of his hand even before he has put his rod together, melancholy Trefor surveying the waters.

★★★

More than two seasons would pass before I caught a fish, towards the end of my third. As to catching trout, here I don't include the Glen stream, the source of the Lledr, Dulyn stream or Llyn-y-Foel.... I mean at the Black Lake. But you'll know why I loved the stream, and how it saddened me if the men were too keen to get home and wouldn't delay for me, though they'd delay for themselves, or for my father whose stamina or sheer determination outstripped theirs, until night was almost upon us, if it suited, and fish were rising, or might just yet rise, though none had done all day.

Let me pour into your mind all those blank days, at least half if not the majority of them bleak days, wet and cold, and ask you to think of what my tale is told: of stoicism and endurance beyond whose years? Not beyond mine then, resolved into my own invisible self, if beyond them now.

I was too small, too slight, however wiry, to do more than I did by way of fishing the Black Lake, and for safety's sake too bound to fish in my father's wake, where the water was disturbed. I did my best, struggling to cast without my back-cast hooking me up behind, without my line splashing onto the water, without falling in. But really everything was against me. A less determined or peculiar boy might well have decided after a few Sundays that he'd had enough of fishing at the Black Lake. Bugger that, he might have said, for a game of soldiers. But not yours truly. I could absorb any amount of such punishment, being captive to the dream and standing oblique to the everyday world already, maimed by it. As my life at school had shown. So much for 'Schooling':

Pay attention at the back there.
But the back of the mind knows better.

If it didn't where would I be,
and who, empty of all poetry?

Once

***

People who don't know tend to think all fishing is sitting on a bank waiting for a fish to bite. But fly-fishing is one of constant activity, of casting and retrieving, and re-casting, zipping the line back out, through the full 180° of the shore, or as near to that as obstacles, in this case the rocks, allow. There was not a single stunted shoreline thorn or mountain ash to hinder you at Dulyn, or for a trout to feed under either. So you work methodically through the arc, eighteen inches by eighteen inches, or yard by yard, as you judge or the winds permit, retrieving the line by drawing it back in short lengths, letting it fall at your feet, or coiling it in your hand. Then by mounting motion, flicking the rod to and fro, you let the line shoot out again, with a minimum of casts.

You don't want to thrash the air, or whip the water. That will disturb any fish that might be in the swim, near the surface, feeding perhaps, or hunting for food, or hanging with minimal motion in mid-water, at some preferred place, where natural food washes by, or is stirred up by a feeding streamlet. The little flies dart forward as you draw the line back a few inches at a time, or at whatever speed you feel is 'lifelike'. Their movement catches the trout's eye. The trout 'rises' to take the fly.

Or so it goes in theory. But circumstances alter cases: time of year, recent weather, weather on the day, weather in the moment, water temperature, wind temperature, wind-direction and force, the flies you chance to try, to stick with or restlessly replace, the delicacy with which your line settles on the water, the speed you retrieve at, your ability to sustain concentration, to cast methodically, at the right range, in the right place, for which you need an eye to know, and practice, to identify, to read the water. Then you must do that all morning, moving along from place to place, as the arduous terrain permits; all afternoon, all evening. For if your line is not on the water, what will you catch but thin air?

To do so much as begin, for the first hour, you must find your rhythm and measure and minimise your effort, until you discover you are on automatic pilot, in a trance of motion, your own casting motion and the motion of the waters in the warp of the weather and the turning day, yet vigilant and ready for a trout's sudden swirling take.

Like the waves in the water you have your peaks and troughs, your fallings off and your rising up, especially if you see a fish rise nearby, but mostly without such encouragement. You must manage your mind and your body, as you'd do in a race across country. But at ten years old, at eleven and twelve, in torrential mountain rain and whipping wind? Or even on a fair day of ideal conditions? With no encouragement from the fish, not a sign or a chance all day? Minute upon minute, hour upon hour? And every discouragement as your father catches his first and then his second and his third, and Ifor, when you meet up, has six fish in his polythene bag, and you are no better than Trefor, except your line isn't out and sunk from view with a worm on the end of it. For there is also competition in it, for the sake of self-esteem. Such strife is good for mortals, as someone said. If hard on ten-year- olds?

★ ★ ★

How many trips it took me to become a philosopher in my apprenticeship, I cannot say. For boyhood hope springs eternal, and when its spring has sprung, disappointment follows hard on it, and crestfallen sorrow settles in. Presumption is ever followed by despair. But little by little unconsciously I displaced it. The present became my experiment, the discovery of the present.

I became a conscious and unconscious naturalist in one. My fishing bag and even SCOTIA became props in another adventure, my cover story, to serve a parable-maker one day; and perhaps this was why I didn't catch a fish sooner? I spent more time fishing half-heartedly while staring into the soul of things, of sight and sound, as the unmeasured hours blew across the bowl of sky above the rocky cauldron and its black, black-hearted lake.

In such a place it would be profoundly wrong to say nothing happens. A wilderness lake is like a wild island inside out. For me it was a training ground for Inis Mór and the incantation of reverie. As no-one knows better than I do now, what happens in such places happens differently, at another pace, on a different plane. The seasons rotate. Days lengthen and shorten but the prevailing direction is round like the shore of the lake – longest way round, shortest home – and sometimes up and down. Our day is only a day and not the devil but the bounty is in the detail.

Winter fills what summer drains, or at least so it was in the old dispensation. Water temperatures rise a degree or two and fall. Trout rise. The ring-ouzel haunts the heath on the cliff and flits up to perch in the rowan to sing, if song you'd call it. Mist descends. For half the day it hangs and drifts mizzling about the cliffs. What happens is of that order. In time your mind registers, weathers in it, as a stone weathers and records its weathering.

I became consciously a survivor, a scavenger, pausing to gather tinder, dry heather stalk and bits of wave-washed wood and other combustible waftage, jammed under rocks. Where did it come from? It was hard to imagine. But there was always a supply, though it thinned out through the season. I looked ahead to the brew and the baked-bean feast. I looked ahead to fire and warmth. I looked ahead to these things as I lay in bed waiting for my father to rouse.

Or as I listened to the wind and rain at my bedroom window, I feared the day and lamented my fate. There seemed no middle way between lamentation and hope, fear and hope. On cold days the action in fishing kept you warm. Fire was the only other thing that might, apart from a brown trout rising to your cast. But how long must I wait? I would try to read the day ahead on the ink-wash air of dawn, what my great-grandfather called the 'carry', as we left the house, whether it would be wet up there or cold, or fair, and as we drove towards the Conwy revise my opinion.

When we moved to live under the Wooded Hill you could see the mountains from the house, even as you brushed your teeth, and through the week take the measure of your doom as Sunday approached. But you could never be sure, for a sudden change of wind direction might bring rapid and icy rain, as the clouds crash-landed on the mountains, or peat-soft soddening drizzle, as the mist rolled down, fuming. So low it might fall it could seem as if it rose from the lake. Then every sound was hugely amplified, every sheep-bleat or cough, every bird-call, and the tumbling and dashing of water roared. These were the mood-swings of god. Once on such a day I watched an immature peregrine falcon stoop and stoop on an immature herring gull, dashing it into the lake, and dashing it again as it rose, playing with it, cat-and-mouse, practising, for how long I do not know but it seemed all morning.

But once at least, after a day at Caw Lwyd, I saw the real kill, and benefitted from it:

All day fishing there I waited as much for its shrill *kek-kek-kek-kek kek-kek* and scimitar soaring overhead as for the dimpling fish below.

How the day might plod on otherwise, the water hypnotic, light falling like manna, and all slap-happy in the rocks.

Every plane and facet of wave-mirror and cliff-hanging
edge of expectancy, pitched there, in and out of the dream.

What sense trying to address the future? Whatever it contains
won't include us. The art of waiting its métier as mine.

Once as we came back on an autumn evening, weary for the road,
school to face in the morning, homework not done, down one raced

in his scholar's gold rim glasses, and tear-smudged eye from too
much study,
and thumped a grouse into the heather. Then, wings winnowing

and alarmed *kek-kek* for cry, it shot away, leaving us its prey,
the bird warm where we found it, severed from its head.

How much out of ten might I get for that? At fourteen, mind-
wandering,
learned only in the progress of the clock, in a world beyond time.

As we drove and as we marched to the Black Lake, I would
be thinking of my favourite corners, and the one I loved
best of all, the tiny northwest bay, right under the cliffs, fed
by little streams, from waterfalls down the black rockfaces.

In time when I could spend the day on my own this is
where I'd head, and I'd not pause at all on reaching the lake,
but say goodbye to the men, and hike as fast as I could, and
then come upon it quietly, slip into it, as if it was as natural
for me to be there as it was for the dipper bobbing on a rock
in the middle of a steep and gushing streamlet, or for the
sudden peregrine, flashing its crescent across the sky, and
crying *kwaahk-kwaahk-kwaahk* and *kek-kek-kek-kek*, as it
soared breakneck to disappear among the precipices.

The peregrine was the rarest of sights in the 1950s, DDT
having soared up the food-chain, at the top of which it
perched, knocking off contaminated pigeons until the
peregrine could no longer reproduce. I longed every day I
was there, for a sight of it, or failing that to hear its cry. I'd

crane my neck the moment I heard it for just a glimpse of its lightning – the 'foreign hawk': 'Hebog Tramor' as the Welsh name has it, and as I once called a poem about seeing the peregrine in Manhattan's Upper West Side:

Once the falcon fell from hearing,
from the top of the food chain,
as the DDT rose in its bloodstream.
And man held his dominion
over the world below.

The falcon could not hear the falconer.
But the centre held as once its talon.
Where did the falcon go?
Like a people uprooted forever
and no store set until too late?

I used to crane my neck to see him
thinning the mountain air
and marvel at the way he'd sheer
two steep seconds off the moor,
quicker than you can say fate.

Now I crane to see him again
spiralling round the 'God Box'
centre for world religions in New York.
In Welsh 'the foreign hawk',
as if looking for a way in.

But other bird presences at the Black Lake laid claim to me too and held me spellbound: the raven rolling overhead calling *cronk-cronk*; the ubiquitous wren, weaving its bold story, in and out of every nook and cranny, and declaring its regal heritage, singing to itself, with the loudest and most piercing song, big enough to deafen a mountain; or the melancholy ring-ouzel in its clerical bib with its *rat-a-tac-tac-tac* warning, its hellfire sermon; and the dipper – in Welsh *aderyn du'r dwr*, the blackbird of the water – again submerged on the spill of golden gravel where the little stream falls into the lake, the dark waters limpid when the light is right and the wash of waves small, the dipper dining, on caddis larvae. I could find myself so close to it – find myself indeed – I could see its little rusty bib, like the blush of rusted iron in granite in those mountains.

The dipper shares its call and song with the wren: clink-clink, tap-tap-tap, as of two pebbles struck together rapidly, and then the quicksilver warbling. So if you hear either you must turn to be sure which one it is. In Welsh the dipper shares its name with the ouzel – the blackbird of the water, which is unusual in a language so tending to specificity in naming. Then the stonechat, the wheatear, the meadow-pipit... the cuckoo on the skyline.

Something in me fell for these birds. My heart in hiding? Every time I saw one it was the first time, as for the trout itself. I couldn't watch them or stare into them too long. They made time fly as much while they sat still as when they flew. The streamlets here filled the sound-scape, folding you in so well you seemed to be contained in a bubble with the birds that came and went about their business, oblivious or careless that you were there, in their dwelling-place, beside the lake's wide eye, its heavenward gaze. A gaze that trafficked in light. Nowhere else except fishing from rocks by the Atlantic have I felt so much caught up by the aura of water. Nowhere until that adventure had I so sustainedly studied durance and endurance and learnt my place in the world.

I became absorbed into the physical intimacy of the place itself more generally, the rocks, the stones, the slabs and cliffs, and the colour in them. They were never black and never grey but the light fell on them differently and the rain washed them, and as the seasons shifted ground, from spring to autumn, the foliage changed hue, and impressions of the place mutated. They mutated by the moment and once you saw that, whether you knew you were seeing it or not, you were more finely absorbed into the soul of the place, and the nursing air and the elements became you.

Not only were there the sounds of tumbling streams and of the wind, but also the bleat of sheep, the occasional cough echoing, sounding almost human. Sheep used to graze on the crag in dizzyingly impossible places. Sometimes you'd see one fall, bouncing once or twice, to its death. Sometimes you'd discover by your nose alone, one that had fallen since your last visit.

All this was something I never felt more powerfully than when my head hit the pillow at the end of the day and for a moment the whole world I'd been in, rolled and plunged about me, as if reluctant to let me fall into the underworld of sleep, or else to ease my fall, with all the sights and sounds in which the day had held me entranced, suspended from the world and its business. It was like falling out of one dream, and into another, in the dark of the night ahead, where other days stir fecund.

So my first love affair began, and like the course of true love, like life itself, it had its trials and sorrows, its heartbreak days, its moodswing frustrations and minor dramas.

★ ★ ★

We'll move on. For we have some way to go, some years to travel, round this water and the world might otherwise be over before we get there.

We'd move on, in my first times there, most often by the southerly shore, westward, to the last bay on that southwest side, parted from what became my beloved northwest bay by the highest and most massive cliffs. While my father would climb the spur of cliff and disappear down to ledges where he might fish, I must go by 'The Eye of the Needle'.

This was the narrowest and lowest of passages, with irregular steps, cut out under a huge natural lintel. As to incline, it was hard to get an extended fishing rod through it. As to width, the full bulk of a man, rich or poor, and his fisherman's trappings were a squeeze. The 'Eye' and its steep steps led you up through the rock, and onto the bluff there, from which you could see the whole lake before you, except that immediately below, where my father fished, invisible but for the flashing tip of his rod or the sight of his darting line, and I would wait up there, for however long he might be, waited and above all stared.

And that would be the way the day went, except where I could get safely down to the water, as soon became possible, the cliffs stepping back and a kind of green and rocky world opening up, to a shallower shore, fed by a stream. But the better fishing lay in the steep small dark bays farther on, leading to the cliffs themselves and their sheer drop into the lake. Here we'd often spend the day, leaving the other shore to Trefor and Ifor. Such was the distance and the rocky nature of the shore, that you could rarely see where the others were, tiny figures not a fingernail high. The place absorbed us, our figures lost by distance and the camouflage of angular and rounded rocks that broke our shapes. And our dreams absorbed us. For long passages of the day, we were so much there it was as if we weren't there. We weren't dreaming, we were the dream. We didn't think. Therefore we were drawn into life.

Here I would look to prepare a hearth and lay a fire in a nest of rocks, for a mid-morning brew, for a lunchtime of *Swiss Knorr* packet soup, and *Heinz* baked beans and little sausages out of the same tin, to put some warmth in us. I liked to have the makings of the fire in hand before too long, and would clamber up where the heather grew, or delve among the shoreline rocks for jetsam, bevelled bits of wood, tinder dry.

Allow that it didn't rain all the time, if you will. But I remember those wet days as if they are recorded in my bones. To think of them reminds me of the way a prisoner ticks off the days of his sentence, one by one. How a plastic cup of soup could seem like manna from heaven. How a stew of baked beans and sausages and lumps of the heavy, dense brown bread my mother made warmed the cockles of our hearts, in the pelt and shiver of the Snowdonian heavens let loose, for a day. These were times I especially loved, in solidarity with my father. I liked to feel myself a boy-man, in tough comradeship, refusing to let hardship get the better of me. My hands would be blue with cold and the undersides of my fingers wrinkled from the icy water off my line and the rain itself. Sometimes on a hard day we'd be restless and soldier back the way we came, perhaps just to get warm, and by chance meet Ifor and on occasion Trefor, or we'd go to join them, brew some tea together, and curse the weather and the day we were born.

★ ★ ★

I want you to think it through minutely, minute upon minute, hour upon hour, from a boy's-eye view, first to last, season after season, spring, summer, autumn, year after year.... I want you to imagine how it changed, as I grew older, too, more independent, and more silent, more in my own world, and capable of catching fish.

First catch your trout. So, after an arduous Black Lake apprenticeship, I finally did, in quite spectacular fashion, one very bright late afternoon. The day was an airy one and beautiful and the water full of light, and the radiant rocks sparkling. I fished now with dogged devotion. It was a ritual in which my only thought had become to cast my line to perfection, every time, as far and as thoroughly as I could, all day long, never mind the absence of luck, the apparent futility of it: one must do a thing for its own sake, as best one can. So I do on this page. When a fish rose I would cast to it. But I was unlucky or there was something I was doing wrong, some rhythmic thing about the way I retrieved the fly. Or I got a fish on and lost it.

I was on the overspill. It's not a very wide structure, you must understand, not like a big dam. Twenty feet wide at most, I'd say. There'd been enough rain that year for the lake to spill through spring and early summer, but now it merely brimmed and rarely did a wave lap a foot onto the spill. I stood and cast out into the bay. How many times had I cast my line that day? How many times since that first day of days? How far had I grown into this place that now it did not matter if I did or didn't catch a fish? I'd lost heart to find faith. But then at the very full extent of my range, immediately a fish took my fly. It was so alien a sensation I had to think about what to do.

The hooked fish swam fast towards me, faster than I could retrieve the line, and keep it tight between us. It was as if it knew that by gaining slack it might throw the hook. As frantically I drew line, I stepped back further to counter the trout's advance, and back, and... fell down onto the next level of the overspill. I suppose a two-foot fall, but when you aren't expecting it, and you have your first Black Lake trout on the end of a line, caught on a fly of your own tying, it's not just a comic distance, it's a deep, heartbreaking fall through all eternity, slow-motion, bruised and grazed, S Scotia's varnish itself grazed. But I bounced back immediately. Sprang up those two feet as if I'd never fallen, as if immune to gravity.

Rewind fast, play it backwards and back I am rewinding. I rewound and wound at my reel and raised the tip of my rod, against all slackness, slackness of heart about to befall me, but for the miracle that the fish was still there, bringing unmanly tears to burn my eyes, quickly forced back. So trembling, all goose-bumped, I landed him.

'A decent fish,' as I am bound to say.

But a decent fish they all agreed, and not least my father, who'd been fishing just across the bay and saw the whole drama unfold, my starring role, disappearing and reappearing like a jack-in-the-box, still only a slip of boy, slow as I was, slow as I have been to mature and find myself, living too long in the dream-element and not long enough, unfitted for the unknown world to come, but quick as lightning for the kill that afternoon.

There was the trout, a decent fish, of course, from high summer. It was no common common speckled fish, but one of those hard-fighting three-quarter pounders. Not just a fish but the key to all others, the key to self-belief. It wasn't that now the trout fell over themselves to be caught by me, but that I knew I had the measure of them. The lake had played with me as the falcon played with the gull. But now I had the measure of the Black Lake and from that moment on, I held my own. As I grew stronger, I could fish harder and cast my line farther, and now I was ready to begin to study the trout itself, and to learn the water intimately as a fisherman.

So it was, and so I toiled and grew, through thick and thin, fair weather and foul, on our pilgrimages to the Black Lake, and passed into a whole other way of being. Our time there then was our 'Paradiso':

> It was discipline and fleetness of mind
> and footwork in the old metres carried
> the day up there, those days bedazzled
> by sun and cloud running on the wind.
> The poets prolific in all they touched,

quick to hook their lines into the rising
poems, whether at dawn, midday or evening.
They could do nothing wrong. And it seemed

Wales was theirs forever, rain or shine.
No one came up that far but if he did
they knew him without looking twice,
come over the top from nearer heaven
and shared a brew and said, word of god,
they'd find no better day in paradise.

It's not that I didn't grow up with my peers, at least not
latterly. As to that, as we grow we all maintain a distance,
variably, as we discover ourselves and each other. It was that
once a week in the season I looked at things from a different perspective. That conditioned me. I took naturally to
solitude and inwardness like a duck to water. As if I was
inside the words at last, one and the same with meaning.
And I could be uncomfortable in company, preferring not
my own, but the absence of all company, be it at the stony
limits or at home under the wooded hill. The Black Lake
time was about a place, a unique place (as all places are
unique), and it was about the brown trout. But it was also
and no less about being-in-the-world and about the dream
and the poem. So it was for my mentors and comrades,
John, Ifor and Trefor, each in our way. It helped render me
unfit for the world's work, or played to that strength in me
that would not, could not, subscribe to the lie in the midst
of life.

By the time I was seventeen I discovered a different kind
of watershed from those I'd known in the mountains. Quite
as suddenly as a fish rises to the fly, I fell smitten by the
history master's raven-haired daughter. A year my senior,
too, and so apparently beyond attaining, she soon took all
my thoughts and dreams. So that, at first, as I fished those
latter days with John and Trefor and Ifor my mind ran not

on trout but on her alone. I imagined her seeing me, especially when I caught a fish. I imagined her admiring me, wirily resolute in the wilderness, in the mountaineer's stout Dolomites that eventually replaced my father's boots. But was she even aware of my existence? Oh yes, I'd caught her eye, I knew. Though I didn't know what to do about it. Nor did I know but here began my downfall and my ruin, on the road to the unknown world.

That was all after we'd moved to live under the Wooded Hill, to the other corner of the triangle's baseline, and late in the day there.

With the Welsh girl in possession of my heart, another kind of distance grew between me and the Black Lake. And it caused me to renounce my past, for the duration. But any such renunciation is as illusory as 'in love' itself and the intoxications of such passion. I knew that past so well, so intimately, in every corner, by every rock, in every light, and in all weathers, it was always there to haunt me again, a seduction, a comfort, a mode of being, a deep well of recollections, sights and sounds, a natural history, a place to weather in, to retreat to in the face of adversity and setback, black ink in my inkpot, a ground and grounding, a sheet-anchor, a drogue, forever after: the apex of my triangulation in those years and still so in the map of being, as if it was written in my DNA.

* * *

When my father died, it was the first place I found him haunting in my mind's eye. There he went disappearing to the far corner, hard to make out, fishing resolutely all day. He haunted me like a lost love, and also with the vigour of guilt. And there was some guilt in that I had wavered in our common faith and devotion to the common speckled fish, all for a beautiful Welsh girl. (Whom I'd betray. Who'd betray me.) There was guilt in my beholdenness for those nevermore times and the gift they were, but that was a distortion of mourning and not to be borne. It bears repeating: life is all becoming and time is new everyday, however short our future on earth.

And here for a footnote, as to becoming and the world going its way. Not two weeks after my father died, at 85, an impulse at a newstand led me to pick up and browse a copy of *Trout and Salmon* magazine. This isn't something I'm at all in the habit of doing. I don't like the idea of fishing as sport or leisure and all that goes with it, the fishing 'business'. To me all that is a travesty of what commonly is called nature. For me fishing is no-nonsense spiritual engagement with nature and eternity. But something prompted me, and what did I open it at but a double-paged colour photograph of the Black Lake, from high on the hill, above the track down from Melynllyn, a view right round from the overspill to my favourite northern corner, the perspective and wide-angle ironing out the precipitous nature of the cliffs, the steepness of the shore, but showing the lake as black as I've led you to believe it to be. Scoop some of it up in your hand and be surprised to see it's transparent, not black at all, though the ink in my ink-bottle looks no blacker.

'Trout where the ravens fly' the article was called. It told of one Gary Lyttle's trek into the Welsh hills, in search of wild brown trout, and declared that 'Dulyn enjoys a spectacular location'. And here I read how things had changed: the lake had been stocked with char, and with 'native' trout from Brenig reservoir. The one-pound fish held across Gary Lyttle's outspread hands was clearly one of these stocked fish, not native for a moment. I could have told you that as a boy, except there were no stock fish in the Black Lake then, and never a char, but only true native dark-backed common speckled fish, *brithyll* – monoglot trout as old as Wales – *brithyll du*, you might say. But heartening it was to see the double-spread photograph, and to have the article's author confirm how hard he'd had to toil to reach the lake. That's something time is unlikely to change too much, unless we evolve to sprout wings and to fly. My father had only just died. Was it his spirit prompted me to pick up that magazine? I'm not given to such superstition. But the occasion made me wonder. It was a magazine he regularly bought. The fishing 'business' didn't deter him.

But haunt me, he did, and does. I fish for trout more now than for many a year since those days in my youth. But not, I am sorry to say, for too many years at Dulyn. Here, as a footnote to my footnote, is a poem my father's death prompted from me. I call it 'Gone for Good':

> How many more poems will you haunt,
> old man? I know you won't say, but
> don't pretend you're not keeping count.
> I know you and I know you're not done yet.
> As on those endless dour days you'd cast
> and cast into the evening and keep casting
> while I'd pray the next would be your last
> not knowing then that faith is everlasting.
>
> My mother said you just upped and left
> but that was ever your way, if you could.
> Given half a chance to fish I'd do the same.
> There's nothing new except we are bereft
> and now we say you've gone for good
> which so far hasn't lived up to its name.

But he was alive and in his prime when his father died and we inherited the house under the wooded hill, *Tan-yr-Allt...*

Whither, to another part of the wood: *exuent omnes*.

THE WOODED HILL

Not all headlands aspire to the condition of islands. But the Great Orme, as the Norse name is, or Gogarth as Welsh prefers – St Tudno's headland – at the end of the Creuddyn Peninsula, was surely once an island. And it might become one again, with a little help from climate change in due time. If that happens it will fulfil an apocalyptic fantasy of my youth, in the name of small islands and their beauty. What still attaches and detains the Orme lies below sea-level but not yet below the sea.

In my day the Creuddyn isthmus – the name connotes bloodiness, after massacre – was for much of its length a delta of green farmland, with the town huddled and piled up a little at the end of it, taking a foothold where it might on the lower landward terraces of the Orme's head. There, in winter, on the plain, flashes of flooding would surface to blink at the sky. These sudden surfacings, uplifting to heart and eye, most of all on a whistling-cold morning, were haunted by gulls and waders, oyster-catcher, curlew, sandpiper. They were a breath of fresh air and I loved the way they brought a frisson of shoreline landward of the town.

What caught me then and catches me now is the way such manifestations, such upwellings, expose the tenuous nature of our settlement. How easily it might go down, and be as nothing. Such flashes come to life most at dawn and nightfall, spring and winter, with change of light. So in youth and age *tempus fugit* inspires impatience and scorn at human vanity.

If only we could grasp our insignificance and live appropriately. Getting and spending we lay waste our powers. Little we see in Nature that is ours. So runs the text. It's only a matter of time before souls become extinct, as I put it in a strange poem written in 1968 on Inis Mór: the soul is only human after all.

Edge-of-town supermarkets and new housing occupy those open spaces now. The flash-floods are drowned out by Asdaville and shopping 'parc', tarmac and concrete. The ground remains below sea-level, protected so far by sea-wall-cum-promenade. But there is hope yet, post-apocalypse, to name Ynys Gogarth or Tudno... or Inis Orme, Orme Island, the Isle of Orme, as anyone left alive might choose. Ferryman wanted.

My Scottish grandparents are buried on the Great Orme. They lie in a graveyard – O grave yard – whose cross-eyed northerly aspect squints up the Irish Sea, beyond the Isle of Man, to Galloway, home from home, for my grandpa at least (my granny was born in Govan). An ideal lodging, in the circumstances. Who wouldn't prefer self-draining limestone to dank and wormy clay? I did not go to either funeral. I was deemed too young, even at twelve, my age when grandpa died. It was his death, my granny predeceased him, that brought us seven miles west along the coast to live at Tan-yr-Allt.

The house stood at the eastern boundary of Llandudno, high above the town, 'under the wooded hill', as so expressively the Welsh name has it. Where do you live? Under the wooded hill....What a way to think and speak. Hard to think too at this point in my legendary ideal story that only ten years later I'd be living on Inis Mór (too mundanely, the big island), another limestone landscape to praise, living out my dream for real, or unreal, playboy of the western world. So this time under the wooded hill nursed the dream and helped it grow. What was the dream? That our lives are travesties, whatever our dreams. Or are dreams are travesties, whatever our lives? I know what I believe.

From our vantage beneath the cliffs, we oversaw the known world, 180° of it anyway, wild Wales and beyond, from the Carneddau and supporting cast – Black Lake country – in Eastern Snowdonia to the Isle of Man itself (a speck on a very clear summer's evening), taking in Penmaenmawr, Ynys Môn (Anglesey) and Ynys Seiriol (Puffin Island *aka* Priestholm), across the Conwy estuary, and the Great Orme, in a single westerly panorama of chastening beauty.

Though before you get carried away, I should say too that the panorama included, slap in the middle of the picture-postcard, the town's rusty gasometer and the rubbish tip. Over the tip yellow bulldozers sailed all day like trawlers on high seas. Beyond them according to the tide, year in year out, real old-style wooden-hulled trawlers came and went in the estuary, haloed by gulls as they ran home, their Ailsa Craig engines beating like my heart to see them from my high vantage point. Fare forward! What kind of youth was I, to be so hooked? What was written into me to set my course like that?

Gulls wheeled about the bulldozers to strengthen the sea-going simile, and flew in their wake, raucous airborne litter, day-in-day-out, a billowing conflagration, burning intensely at sunset, in summer from the wooded hill. In the middle ground, the gasometer went up and down like an iron lung, according to the tides of consumption and supply, high and low water, breathing in sea-air corrupted by the tang of refuse, endless garbage from the town's hotels. But it was all beautiful to me, the salt air and the windy town, the mountains, the islands, the estuary and the running sea: my province to find beauty in ugliness. Why wouldn't it be?

For Nature is everything and nothing without the human entanglement. Or who'd sing and celebrate it and all its wonder and waste? Who'd pay it homage? Apart from the shorebirds with their starry chatter, the song-thrush in the dark wood, the blackbird – those immortals of our parish? Though you'll hear them sing out of season more often now, thrown out of kilter as they are by their body clocks. Wind them on, wind them back. What's happened to the Spring?

★ ★ ★

Here and now, under the wooded hill, we were confirmed in our unbelonging: cultural and social borderers, within and without the town, newcomers, 'Mcs' not 'aps'. We'd stepped from Denbighshire into Caernarfonshire. This was a marked difference most simply expressed in terms of Sunday opening. Our Sundays must now be dry. We were in hellfire Wales proper, if with limestone not brimstone. Though that hardly concerned me then, as to drinking. By the time it did, the populace had voted, or was on the brink of voting, to join the twentieth century, good or ill.

Had we not moved, and at the very threshold of my teens, it always strikes me hard how my life would have been utterly different. My social roots would have been stronger. I would have been a different person, with quite other stories to tell of that time, and I'm sure even as to subsequent adventures. So vital and determining was it, and for me at least, so perfect in its timing: as I left boyhood behind and embarked on youth, wildly unworldly by today's standards, but an honest-to-god sinner in those times. So chance makes us and becomes choice, or seems to. Who was it said those who voyage across the seas change their skies but not their souls? (The poet Horace.) But my soul underwent a sea-change none the less and how could it not with the skies the way they were now in our westerly and northerly seascape?

Not that uprooting from the Red Wood didn't have its hurts. Nor was it complete, for my father still worked there, and we always kept our family friendships there, and knew great ties in heartening reciprocity of affection.

Like the Red Wood too, the wooded hill was a place of jackdaws. They nested on the cliff, they nested in our chimney, and cackled continuity, immortal markers always in my mental map. So it is even as I hear them in the evening now in suburban middle England, flying in loose flocks home to roost, wherever home might be for them here, not down our chimney, anyway. Homage to them, local shades, and their sudden blissful crescendi and shimmer above the wooded bryn.

Not that coming to a new school didn't have its traumas. Flashbacks from my original educational shellshock disturbed me at John Bright Grammar School. There I found my education much less advanced than that of my fellows. I was behind in everything, except cross-country running. Even in English, otherwise my only academic salvation, I lagged. For here it was more about drawing columns and parsing sentences than anything else. You hardly saw a poem or read a book or had a chance to write an essay in those middle years, and there lay my emerging interest, blessing or curse, my only possible salvation.

For a while, I couldn't work out what on earth they were doing. It was disturbingly like not being able to read. I regressed into that earlier hypnotised-rabbit state caught in the headlights of what I couldn't construe. Such misery. The shade of it can hover about me even now, if I have to do anything remotely testing with numbers. I can feel my ears burn this minute at the mere thought of it.

I knew then what a sentence was, and an adjective: a thing to purge, according to my father, and an adverb, and so on. Writing is just what's in your mind, he'd say. You don't need to know any of that. Though damn me for a fool when an end-of-term report suggested I took him at his word. But even when you roughly got the hang of it, filling columns, treating sentences as if they were formulae in chemistry, was the soul of boredom. What was the point of it? What was the point of any of it – the so-called education? I preferred chemistry. I did very well in chemistry. How on earth I do not know. In reality though I preferred the word, spoken and heard. As I do now. But now I add the printed word, as the alpha and omega of all.

On Mondays, in the trout fishing season, I'd sometimes be so tired anyway and distracted by the reverie of yesterday and the promise of next Sunday, there was very little I could work out at all. I spent a lot of lesson-time in speculation, in considering the ways of the brown trout and the secrets held along the shores of the Black Lake. Nor was my homework likely to have been done.

If I wasn't daydreaming about trout, it would be about a hare I'd seen that sudden frosty morning, in the low field, quite unusual to see there. Or it was a pheasant that had rocketed into our wood from next door. Would it be there – somewhere to intuit and stalk in the fading light – when I got home? Or in winter when snow fell in the hills I'd rehearse how I'd steal up on the woodcock I knew to be haunting the bottom of the dark wood, as soon as school was over and I could hurry home.

The school I now found myself in had no time for that

kind of thing. I don't suppose any school ever had, not even a hedge school, the only kind of school I've ever liked the sound of. More hedge than school, I'd hope. It was a highly ambitious school and gave no resting place to the idle dreamer, nor so much as a hint of laurel for the proud scholar to rest on. Not that it ever told us much about John Bright himself. You'd never have guessed he was a radical deeply reviled by the establishment of his day. That might have been something encouraging to know.

But it liked the high-minded association with Mancunian Liberalism and being on the right side of the Corn Laws. That is: the wrong side to the powers that were, with some gesture of sympathy implied, at least, for those who perished in the Great Hunger. Virtue with the benefit of hindsight is all too easy. But I suppose it's better than its opposite. None the less, every year the school sent people to Oxbridge, in the best Welsh tradition, builder's son, butcher's son... nurse's daughter.

In my year and the years immediately above and below, they schooled future professors of botany and history, medical consultants, lawyers, doctors, in considerable number, relative to the local population. They even schooled me, far better than I knew or wanted to believe, holding me back a year that I might develop and come to my senses. Which is a nonsense to say in my case. For I needed to come away from my senses, from my intense sensual pleasure in the world about me, if I needed anything, that is. An institution is only the sum of its individual representatives at a given time. Not even its sum. Only one of all the schoolmasters I suffered under had a life-altering effect on me, and that was the late J.K. Warburton (a graduate of Emmanuel College, Cambridge) who introduced me to the nineteenth-century French writers, the poets especially, Baudelaire above all. He used to say he slept with a portrait of Baudelaire pinned to his bed-head. He was a bachelor, a Methodist lay-preacher, a gay man at a time when it was illegal to be so and lead a fulfilled life.

By way of salvation, right on my first day, I found myself in a class with an older youth, Michael-John Thomas – they were all older youths and older girls; girls always being older in mind than youths, and my birthday falling in August: they'd never look twice at me, no matter how many times I looked at them.

Himself a transplant, from the South Wales valleys, Mikey-John was a great sea-fisher. By chance we'd already met fishing on Colwyn pier the summer before. He was just short of a year my senior. We'd hit it off at once, both of us fanatics for fish, swapping local knowledge, telling tall tales about how good the fishing was in our respective territories.

His fishing already extended to Anglesey, and Llandwyn Island. I was still in the nursery compared with him, with his tales of tope- and conger-fishing... and skate as big as grand-pianos, in the deeps at the far reaches of Llandudno Bay. The happy accident didn't help my studies, but it improved my fishing no end to have a local guide to the estuary and the Orme, a youth who went on to work in the fisheries at Conwy. His approach to fish and fishing even then was much more an exercise in field science than an intuitive shot in the dark of Davy's locker, dreaming under the heavens, such as I preferred.

Apart from Trefor Samuels, Mikey was the first South Walean I ever got to know, he and his mother who worked for her mother in the general store on the council estate. I recognize now, there was a different kind of sociability to them and solidarity, and so with Mikey's South Walean stepfather, who worked in the Junction at Hotpoint. Trefor had it too, lighting his fag in the mountain rain, a warmth first and last. They showed they liked you. They put the human first, in all its fallibility. 'Macky' the Thomases called me, and 'Macky-boy', until it became universal in the known world. To begin with my family looked askance at Mikey's turquoise luminous socks and black winkle-pickers, at the expense of the soul within. But they took him to their bosom in the end.

★ ★ ★

Unlike the one in the hymn, ours was not a green hill exactly. It was literally a wooded hill, or more properly a cliff and a bluff, limestone scarp with outcrop cliffs, terraces, rough grasses, gorse, larch, and thorny scrub. Nor was it far away. I could see it from the schoolyard, and in some cases the classroom. The wood itself, though, was largely evergreen, but the green was broken, relieved by a limestone backdrop, a stone full of brightness and glare, on sunny days above all, and moonlit nights, and never dour but only a little drab in rain.

Great Norwegian pines, forty foot high and more, swept in a tide, a turbulent strait, round the base of the hill. They filled out, up beyond our cottage, into a deep, steep wood, an evergreen sea, a sea-chasm, where the cliffs fell back raggedly, to form the wood's high margin. It was a high and for much of it a very steep wood, petering to a little strand of sporadic hazel, ash and yew, along the southerly boundary, and at its topmost southeast corner, where the tawny owl liked to roost in the ivy.

Not that the wood was coterminous with the property to the east. A little more ground, rough and stony and steep, clambered beyond it to the back wall, the land's most open border, in regular need of repair against our neighbour's wandering sheep. Farther back still from the wood's northern edge, putting an L-shape in our boundary, rose an isolated outcrop of wind-bent larches and pines, Tam O'Shanter Scots pines among them, bonnets set askew by the prevailing westerlies. This wild planting was more-or-less hemmed in by gorse and bramble entanglement and penned back to right-angled walls, the outermost cape or point to our territory.

It was a good place to go if you wanted no one to find you. As I often wanted no one to find me, I was often there. It was a hard place too from which to dislodge wily sheep. The jay tended to skulk here, and the magpie made a nest. Quite often on a warm day a cock pheasant would pick his way in and sun himself beyond the far gorse, a challenge to stalk him there. The place was like a little island, remote, and rarely visited, unless by the sheepdog from the pig farm that neighboured us near there.

Next, beyond, in this back-country lay the disused gulf of Nant-y-Gammar limestone quarry, and farther round, a continuation of our limestone seascape, the Little Orme. Also across that direction but hidden from view, the high village of Pen-y-Bryn where nearly every householder was a pigeon fancier. These men were like poets in their passion for the homing bird. Place-names like Gabowen, Craven Arms and Frome and, beyond the channel: Rennes, La Rochelle, Nantes, Poitiers, Bordeaux... from whence their birds raced home were poetry on their lips and in their hearts.

Pines stood right over our cottage, within a few feet of it at the nearest, and over the yard. Some of them grew straight out of the rock, even out of the face of the cliff itself, having seeded in crannies and grown out and up, crook-handled to the sky.

The cliff immediately behind the house – about sixty feet or so off through the trees at its nearest – was like a land-bound headland, as was another crag in our neighbour's property. More markedly, so was the high-domed bryn known as Fferm. In time, as we observed, the crags of this bryn were colonised by fulmars. Fferm loomed beyond our southern march wall, in Gloddaeth Estate, the demesne of Lord Mostyn. For we had march walls here, on three sides, containing five tilted acres.

Our northern or seaward boundary was discontinuously marked. It ran fenced through a walled orchard, and there was a gate across a path, a strand of barbed wire across a footpath at the very height of the cliff. But no walls make best neighbours, and our neighbours were good neighbours, a family of smiling Christadelphians called Collins. Irish perhaps they were by descent? Kindly folk, they turned the other cheek and a blind eye to a trespassing youth who stalked and hunted pheasants and wood-pigeons and skulked and mooched, and come spring plundered their cliff for herring-gull eggs, as pleased him, in the upper part of what was called 'Collins's Wood', some nine mostly deciduous steep but at the top more open and rolling acres.

The combined properties had once been a single pocket estate, the 'big house' most recently a hotel, our stone-built slate-roofed cottage belonging then to the gardener. In our fiefdom therefore we had an old stone deep-cellared shed called the potting shed, opposite the house, bounding a crazy-paved blue slate courtyard, above which loomed a flotilla of pines. What a thing it was to have a fiefdom, how absorbing and securing. It became part of my consciousness, an outward manifestation of my imaginative life. It haunted me as I went to sleep and in my absences, as at school. I haunted it.

Just beyond the rose-bed there was greenhousing of commercial proportions, including a series of three long, linked, lean-to greenhouses against a plastered wall, and a vinery. Joined together in a 'T-shape', the long greenhouse and the vinery enclosed the top end of an orchard. All a little dilapidated now, they were patched and repaired as best makeshift could do. But the great arterial pipes and the underground boiler-room meant to heat them lay defunct and beyond repair. Yet another big greenhouse stood between the potting shed and the vinery. Here my grandpa had indulged his passion for cacti, and brought on other pot-plants, and it remained for us the cactus house. Who otherwise could never have dreamt of such a thing in our wildest dreams in Red Wood country.

If the greenhouses were serviceable enough, so was the orchard of espaliered apple trees. The staves of wires on which the trees had once been trained were rusted now and broken from their stansions. But gnarled and wired through, reaching out finger-tips to each other, the trees could yet with due pruning fill with blossom in spring and bear more apples than we knew what to do with come autumn. And there were pears a-plenty on trees trained against a sunny stretch of high wall, down beyond the long greenhouse, where my father kept his bees.

These fruit trees and greenhouses stood to the north, seaward of the cottage. They were walled off above the lane by a high wall, in summer topped by that succulent import, red-flowering and white-flowering valerian. The stuff grew anywhere it might seed and root and it flourished in the limestone. So did the great fuchsia, outside our gate, under the gable end of the potting shed. A ground-hugging plant with evergreen leaves and red berries I cannot remember to name claimed much of the lower terrace of the cliff in the same burgeoning fashion.

To the south, inland, below the wood proper, was an area variously used for keeping fowls and growing vegetables. It was skirted by a long hazel hedge running atop a wall, beside a footpath, all that became of the lane at this point, leading, via a stone stile, into the Gloddaeth Estate. Pheasants from the Estate liked to pick along the bottom of this hedge. I was always on the lookout for them and sometimes shot one from the bathroom window, or otherwise slipped from the house to stalk one.

Here, across the way, beyond the little farm, rose the wooded Bryn Maelgwyn, an ancient bardic *allt*, east of Deganwy, itself a legendary location. Both are to be discovered in Lady Charlotte Guest's translations of the *Mabinogion*. But the Maelgwyn and related stories are omitted by modern scholars as belonging elsewhere, not in the branches of those legends. Yet I wish they would provide them anew. For they are a wonder and of the genius of that part of the world, worthy an appendix at least. I could see these places every day when the leaves were off the high hazel hedge, as I stood to clean my teeth. Idle window-haunting filled much of my time. It was a male pursuit in our house, sometimes shared and accompanied by spoken observation. Then at any moment it might become intensely purposeful, as I'd be despatched with the gun, at my father's direction, in the hope of putting one delicacy or another on the menu.

The terrain of Gloddaeth – of the entire known world, in outline anyway – has been described by that intrepid Welsh traveller, and explorer in the Western Isles, Thomas Pennant:

> From hence is a short walk to GLODDAETH... placed on the slope of a very extensive hill, or lime-stone rock.... The upper walks [reaching the heights of Fferm, beyond our wooded hill], having fortunately a steep and stubborn rock for their basis, checked the modish propensity to rectitude; so there was a necessity to deviate from it; but in no greater degree than the flexure of a zigzag would admit. Notwithstanding some blemishes, corrigible at an easy rate,

these walks may be considered among those of the first rate
of this island, for such beauties of view as nature can bestow;
and, from those spots favoured by the sight of *Conwy*, I may
add the majestic ones of ancient art. Every flight of path
presents new and grand objects; first the great windings of
the river towards *Llanrwst*, the lofty towers of Conwy, and
the venerable walls of the town; and beyond is a long extent
of *alps*, with *Moel Siabod*, the *Drûm*, and *Carnedd Llewelyn*
and *Dafydd* [Black Lake country], towering with distin-
guished height. From a little higher ascent is opened to us the
discharge of the *Conwy* into the sea, sublimely bounded by
lesser *Penmaen*, and the immense *Orm's Head*, or *Llandudno*;
between which appear, a fine bay, the vast promontory of
Penmaen Mawr, the isle of *Priestholm*, and the long extent of
Anglesey. After gaining the summit, beneath is seen a considerable flat, with the estuary of the river *Conwy* falling into the
Irish sea on one side, and the beautiful half-moon bay of
Llandudno on the other: one of whose horns is the great head
of the same name; the other the lofty head of *Rhiwleden*, or
the little *Orm's Head*. A little farther progress brings us in
sight of a great bay, sweeping semicircularly the shores; and
beyond are the distant hills of *Flintshire*, and the entrances
into the estuaries of the *Mersey* and *Dee*, frequently animated
with shipping.

Like Robinson Crusoe on his island, we could have
subsisted under the wooded hill, had we really been pressed
to. And for several years we produced and kept more than
we could consume, honey from the honey-bee too.
Asdaville and its like hadn't been invented. We lived a little
closer to nature, but fortunately not out of necessity. My
father still had his day job and wrote and wrote away, books
and journalism, as if there might be no tomorrow, as I often
wished at the end of Sunday, or when the holidays were on
their last legs.

Tan-yr-Allt was a land of milk and honey, except we kept
no cow. It was Eden. Though we toiled and moiled hard
there, for our potato crops, early and late, our peas and

beans, cabbages and sprouts, spinach and leeks, tomatoes, courgettes and pumpkins, squashes and grapes, our fresh eggs, and against the predations of mouse and rabbit, foraging wood-pigeon, egg-stealing jay, magpie and crow.... Wasn't Adam a gardener and didn't he delve? It was paradise gained and full of firewood. It was deliverance from the shipwrecked world. It was heaven on earth, especially to a youth of my inclination, head turned by the Black Lake.

I was now the luckiest person I knew, self-sufficient there in mind too, up the rocky unmade lane, off the last easterly back-road of the town, beyond the pale. My luck would run out at school as you know and I would run adrift there. Yet, to no one's greater astonishment than my own, I passed my exams and got into the sixth form. There ahead of me, a year my senior, and destined for medical school, the history master's daughter could no longer quite look down on me. I'd fallen off the cliff for her the year before. But even as I left the precipice, I knew my passion and devotion were absurd.

At that stage I was as nothing, utterly unaccomplished, disreputable even, one of the 'lads', if a little on the edge of them, by dint of living where I did and being a bit of an odd one. I was young for my years too. So I hope I am still and still postponing to be wise. A scholarly girl, part of the school establishment, a master's daughter, a girl who listened to classical music and played Chopin and Rachmaninov on the piano, who knew her vocation, and so beautiful besides, was hardly going to deign to consider me when she could have her pick of the scholarly boys.

No matter everyday I aligned myself in assembly so that I could fix her with my eye, and steal glances between the heads of other boys, as we sang our hymns: 'There is a green hill far away'... etc, and listened to the announcements.... I was a hobbledehoy who reared racing pigeons, kept a ferret called 'Gorgeous' (who turned out to be afraid of rabbits), reared a pet owl (if one cosmopolitanly named 'Hibou'[*]), procured by a half-gipsy acquaintance who left school early to become a deckhand on the Conwy trawlers. But watch this space.

The bright 'snowcemmed' cottage, cream not white, stood perched high above the lane, rising directly up a fair height from it, its westerly frontage like the side of a fortress. The house itself caught the light. Once you closed the gate behind you, a solid wooden gate too high to see over, affording no view through it, and climbed the slate steps, you left the world and its worries, shut away at your back. There was no need ever to return to either, except the law of the land obliged you to go to school.

Except the estuary beckoned and Gogarth's shore, the Orme's west side, with promise of fish: flounder and plaice, bass and mackerel. The pierhead, too, sang its siren song, a nightfishing song above all, lunging and booming as it waltzed to the tide's motion, like a night out at the Winter Gardens, dancing the conga, and ten sheets to the wind at the Northwestern. It stalked on its centipede legs in the Orme's shadow, wading up to its chest in winter shoals of codling and whiting. Except that from 1 March to 30 September the Black Lake pined for Sunday.

Down below us ran another pinewood in the grounds of a huge crescent-shaped building of grey stone, and glaring orangey-red paintwork, a convalescent home called Lady Forester's, for industrial workers from England (how different their pale dressing-gowned and pyjama'd lives, as you might glimpse them, taking the air on the fire-escape, stealing a smoke). So we had the sea-sound of pine-trees all around, and the sea itself to see at a glance, and to sense in

---

[*] A story told in *But Hibbou was Special* (1964) which called attention to me.

the air, and on wild nights to hear its long drawl, swept up with the roar and crash of pine-masts. On such nights, our bedrooms being in the roof, I'd be rocked to sleep, and startled awake by sudden powerful blasts, and wonder if it mightn't prove my last night on earth. It was very like being at sea, timbers taking the strain, bulwarks and roof-tree, against the house-high waves and crashing breakers of packed air.

We took a westerly and southwesterly full on, and a northwesterly too, even a northerly quite directly. But cold easterlies couldn't get at us at all, though they do their worst, and so we were snug and warm when they blew, tucked up there cozily, safe and sound. One furious night when the wind was in the northwest, some thirty or forty giant pines were levelled down in Lady Forester's. The calamity sounded like the end of the world, just below my bedroom window. A high dormer window, like a lookout in the roof, it always took the brunt of things. Our trees howled and crashed, in great waves running like the sea, but they stood firm, rooted in rock as they were. The greenhouses took a battering, though, with the loss of many panes, and much work to do to repair them as in a poem by Theodore Roethke, brought to harbour at dawn.

Then with the dawn came the aftermath of purest essence, a distillate, in the high tops, the trees thinned of dead branches, the yard and paths and slopes littered with needles and cones, a harvest of kindling thrown ashore. The jackdaws would be cackling as if for the first time in creation, and gulls mewling, and somewhere a pheasant might crow in the wake of the storm, as on summer days you'd hear one, in David v. Goliath style, answering the quarry-blast at Penmaenmawr.

But the air would still be boisterous and billowing, and the sea-horses stampeding, rearing, the morning after the night before, all the way to and fro between Anglesey and our shore, out round the Isle of Man and back, and down the Irish strand by Wicklow where the fishing fleet rode out the night, Frenchmen among them... *L'Etoile, Le Guillemot* and their sisters later known to Seamus Heaney, tuning in to the shipping forecast, just across the sea in Ireland from where we were in Wales: the known world, district and circle.

The wooded hill was not new to me. I had known it from the early fifties, when my grandpa bought the place, on retirement. A blacksmith-next-tenant farmer's son who'd left school in Galloway at fourteen for an apprenticeship on Clydeside, he had since risen in the aircraft industry, to become a production manager for Fairey Aviation and then AVRoe. Now he turned his hand to running his smallholding and like a good Scottish engineer built things to last forever, a henhouse as stout as Noah's ark, a place for them to roam in as secure as a prison yard and as ugly as a concentration camp; and if a thing was broken he repaired it, in the same spirit, calling on my father for labour at the weekends.

There was a peasant's mentality to what he did and a barbarism to his building. Nor would he give us anything but like someone in a story by Maupassant sold us our eggs and wrote the sale up with a pencil in his little notebook. As to landscaping, my father inherited something of his father's blindness. But under our occupancy the brutalism was softened and some more thought given to the look of things.

In grandpa's time, we would go there regularly on a Saturday, or a Sunday in the trout-fishing close season, and have a direct injection of Scotland, under the wooded hill. There wide-eyed I began my explorations and developed my skulking, mooching, stalking, day-dreaming, solitude skills, as brought to perfection at the Black Lake. Where nothing happens, everything begins to happen, nothing being a contradiction in terms.

In those days much more of formality survived to be seen in the grounds. Gardens and pathways echoed something of what Pennant called 'the modish propensity to rectitude', but not without the redeeming 'flexure of a zigzag'. There were garden beds, and just below the big wood, on a terrace, steps led to a sundial. Pampas plumes rose from clumps on either side, like silver-white torches, at the entrance to the dark wood, where I was so happy to be lost. As night fell, how ghostly visible those torches would be: you could use them to steer yourself down the path after a night-time adventure.

Back along the way by the long greenhouse, a blind turret stood above the path. In through the bottom of the wood ran the remains of a chain-link fence, and its gate at the top end, at the wood's southerly entrance, beyond the sun dial, could still be closed, though with difficulty. It was the kind of fence you'd find round a tennis court in the grounds of a country estate. What this one had been intended to keep in, or out, wasn't clear. Now it ran rusted and wrecked under the pines, through clumps of elder.

But the height of all formality and gothic grandeur was the tower at the top of the cliff. You reached it by a zigzag path whose flexure Pennant would have surely approved. It climbed up through undergrowth, round to the south of the main cliff, where the rock dropped back, beside the northerly edge of the big wood. At last it reached a terrace and ran along a couple of hundred yards or so, a little crooked and uneven way, between bramble and scrub, thorn and larch and gorse. By the time it reached almost to the open clifftop, the gorse towered six and seven feet high in places. In wild weather it lunged on the wind and stabbed you in the face and about your head, if you didn't shield yourself with a raised elbow and duck down.

Then you emerged and the known world lay spread out

before you, just as if you were looking down from the window of an Aer Arann plane or a post-war Dakota, bound for Galway or Dublin. The tower commanded the breath-taking view described by Pennant, the full panorama. It was an eyrie, a lookout, a bird's eye view. And it was capacious. You could easily accommodate half a dozen or more people in it, for a picnic. In those early days the remnant of a flagpole survived there.

From the tower you could look down not just on the town – the Naples of the North, with its beautiful crescent bay – and the wider land- and seascape across to Anglesey but also down at wheeling jackdaws and gulls too. And as they swept up you found yourself among them. It was the most exhilarating place on earth. There were the mountains. There hidden away among them was the Black Lake. When my grandpa lay dying in the town's hospital, all exhilaration spent, just beyond the gasworks, we once or twice went up to wave a huge Scottish flag as big as a tablecloth, not the more beautiful Blue Saltire, which was too threadbare to survive the exercise, but the one with the rampant lion, to make him smile, if we could. Though we could not tell if we succeeded.

The tower stood right at the northern boundary of the property. Just a couple of steps beyond its entrance and you entered Collins's wood, my favourite territory. I preferred it partly because it was a mixed wood, largely deciduous, low and wind-combed in its upper reaches. Hunting was better there. And partly I loved it because, strictly speaking, I wasn't supposed to be there, with or without a gun. It was a trespass, and trespass in pursuit of game, I could exaggerate with impunity, yet register the thrill of needing not suddenly to bump into Brian Collins, or his father, so as not to embarrass either party.

Fire a shot in there and watch, and listen, and steal to another part of the wood, lie low and watch, and listen.

Hadn't I read *The Poacher's Handbook* by Ian Niall? Didn't its author bring me up by hand? Let a little while go by unless another opportunity to fill the pot springs up or passes. Then retreat right along the back of the wood, and loiter there as evening falls and the wood-pigeons come to roost, or refuse to. Just so...

> I waited in those days until the evening thinned
> All light away to distant strings and
> Starry clusters, and a green pier-light
> Blowing, like a bird's bright eye,
> Away below, starboard on that seaboard.
>
> It's not that I let anything distract me
> At that wood's edge where I stood sentry.
> Though I heard the odd one flutter home
> Far behind me, and remembered the scent
> Of cropped clover and barley.
>
> And caught a kestrel briefly, anchored at
> The corner of my eye, but kept my watch unblinking,
> Through thick and thin, though rain spat sharply
> And night loomed in. Still they wouldn't come.
> As if something warned them I was there.
>
> I've waited for poems in the same way since,
> At the edge of things, in the heart's dark border.
> And just as shrewdly they've stayed away.
> Though I've caught sight too late
> Of their shadows passing, on the way home.

Or I'd spend the entire day there with the .22 airgun called *Meteor* with its telescopic sight, and make a little fire and cook a blackbird, or a wood-pigeon breast in a piece of foil. Follow your circuit like a fox. Be invisible. Dream of never needing to go home again. Relish nightfall and the winter air descending cold on that beautiful country, sharpening the outline of everything in sight, until night rises up, for it is a mistake to speak of nightfall. Night's of the earth and rises up to fill out shadows as the sun goes down.

By the time we moved in, the formal qualities of the old hotel grounds had fallen a good deal farther from view since the day my grandpa bought his portion of them. Wilderness had taken over more of the place. We kept the paths open, but in a rough and ready way. It was a kind of benign neglect, as far as I was concerned, making it a better place of escape, a better place for bird-life, a better country to stalk. But it wasn't all benign and it wasn't all neglect.

Soon some trespassing youths burnt the remaining stump of the flagpole, and just about as soon, my father converted the tower into a more-or-less impenetrable fortress, its walls coiled with tangles of barbed wire, its entrance barred with a gimcrack portcullis. Theoretically you could raise and lower this great metal contraption through tracks of angle-iron, especially if your name was Hercules, and didn't mind grazing all the skin off your knuckles in the attempt.

It was easier to climb the wall and find a way through the barbed wire. At which I soon became so expert I could do it in the dark. And regularly I had to, but usually only when the very worst storms blew off the coast. For my father, frustrated by our limited television reception installed a TV-aerial up there, elaborately guyed and wedged to hold its alignment to the signal from Manchester or wherever it was it came from in England.

Up until then, down below, under the cliff we were better served by RTE than any other station, something that gave us 'The Riordans' soap opera, the tolling 'Angelus' at six, 'Gay Byrne'... from across the Irish Sea, though we also got the basic BBC. The trouble was no guys or wedges could do anything when a storm hit the cliff head on. Then the aerial would invariably wrench itself out of alignment with all signals. That such winds could be accompanied by lashing rain had nothing to do with the sleety picture-quality or anything that my father heeded. His imperative – as if our lives depended on it – was to restore reception. It was a calamity. So off I'd be despatched, with a heavy mole wrench, a hammer, and a lamp, up to the dark tower, as if I was Childe Harold turned aerial man.

Given the serious nature of the emergency, I paid no heed whatsoever to the long route, but went straight up the cliff, no matter the cold blast and the wild roar of the pines. I'd done it often enough in daylight I could have done it blindfold. First I had to clamber round by the jackdaw's nesting hole, a deep round hole, about the diameter of an apple, created by some flaw in the rock, then struggle on along the first terrace, round up the next step of cliff, often through rainy squalls, and then the second step, more deafening bluster, at last to the tower.

Here the struggle to get in was the more difficult not simply because the coils of barbed wire shook in the wind and were all the harder to negotiate, but because I'd know my father's impatience was itself reaching storm force. I scarcely took time to look out into the storm, to see the town-lights all blurred and blowing, the sea surging, white and broken through the dark, and, perhaps, if the wind was in the west, the bleary lights of a vessel riding out the storm in the lee of the Orme.

Once in the tower the task was to turn the mast into what I guessed was the right position, and to secure it as best I could. The cottage being invisible, away down under the cliff, I had then to climb out, and climb down the first step of rock, to the edge of the next terrace to flash the lamp, requesting a signal. A fully drawn curtain signalled success, a curtain swept impatiently to and fro meant back to the drawing board.

Could the TV be so important? I assure you it could, and every minute lost was viewing never to be recovered, I suppose. So to the dark tower back I came, climbing its wall again, fighting through the barbed wire, getting hooked up on it and scratched by it, struggling with the cold metal mast, hammering and wrenching, not to say swearing, against the deafening wind. Then back down to the ledge again and so on.... What was the code? Was that an opened curtain, way down there? It was no good my father coming out and shouting, as sometimes he chose to. The wind just snatched his voice away, like a hand over his mouth. (How I wished that hand was mine.) You couldn't begin to guess what he was trying to say.

Meanwhile the wind roared, the rain pelted, and abandoned homework festered. The tower wall grazed me, the barbed wire tore me, and the cold metal of the mast and guys numbed my hands, all so that my father might lie on the sofa and watch whatever it was he generally slept through or otherwise condemned as rubbish.

So we settled from the Red Wood under the Wooded Hill, and made our new lives there, complete with grandpa's TV.

★ ★ ★

For me, in those first three to four years, before and as I fell hook-line-and-sinker for the Welsh girl, the wooded hill held me in its thrall. It did so even more than the Black Lake, being on my doorstep, a place more than big enough to disappear in, beyond sight and earshot. It was the dream, the realm of escape, of resolution and independence. No doubt it entailed labour and being at my father's beck-and-call. But that was no price to pay, and I loved it the more the stronger I grew. So the more independent I could be, at working the slope with the two-stroke rotovator, planting the spuds, and so on, thinking on stories of life at North Clutag, authentic peasant life close to the earth. I can think of no happier times, however shadowed by school, however desolate the last day of holiday. There's no mystery in it. What boy primed as I had been wouldn't have felt he had died and gone to heaven under the wooded hill?

There is familiarity and there is intimacy. Intimacy is never familiar but always new. But familiarity can afford it shelter and foster it, as it might foster love. At first to steal from the house with my gun was unfamiliar, an unaccustomed freedom. Before long, gradually, as if stalking step by step, entering that world became like putting on my old army surplus jacket, jeans and boots. I wore the place about me. I smelt of the earth there. It sheltered and fostered me, warped round me as the Black Lake did on Sunday. Black Lake water ran through me, animated me, but this was all present to my eye, each day, school or not.

This was my element. My clothes breathed it. They were worn by it as I wore them, torn, scuffed, grown into the place and earthy. My gun was a tool, an accessory, an extension of me, a talisman. This was especially so when quite soon I graduated to use the Damascus double-barrelled gun my father had used in his youth at North Clutag, a gun discharged by my great grandfather and my grandpa in their day, a twelve-bore gun that spoke to me of many an exploit and occasion. I could lurk cradling it and enjoying it with affection as part of my inwardness.

Talk about worn. Talk about Damascene moments. Its beautiful Damascus steel barrels were paper-thin and would not have survived proofing. They weren't made with modern powder in mind. But my father, I know not how, had hoarded a big cache of black powder wartime cartridges, in old metal ammunition cases, and I used these until I fired the last of them. They weren't too dodgy but sometimes you got a dud that failed to go off. They left more soot up the chimney than their modern counterparts too. Then my father latched on to a lighter modern cartridge that did as well, if no better, except there were no damp squibs. All this reduced the range at which I might knock a wood-pigeon or a pheasant out of the air. In consequence I became a quick snap shot, which suited our tight terrain, if not an exceptionally good shot for the long, deliberate interception. (I had my moments, none the less.)

But the point of it all was I shot for the pot and had the best of whatever I shot, first served, whatever it was, but especially if it was at all exotic, like a woodcock, when I'd have the whole thing to myself, of course. Woodcock are hard to come by. They know the flexure of a zigzag to be sure, when they startle up from the wood floor. But in the evening when they fly in circuits round their territory, in a habit known as roding, they do so steadily, and can be hit more easily. They were scarce, though, scarce as serious snowfall.

Even the pheasants were scarce, unless in the autumn, and after Gloddaeth's first shoots of the season, when survivors sought refuge under the wooded hill and in the grounds below us. The pheasant had to be earned. I became expert in the terrain. Sometimes my father and I would be window-haunting, he talking to me as we stared out, and we'd see a cock bird shoot up and fly away up through the wood, or onto the cliff.

I'd take the angle of it and my father would despatch me, as if I was a dog. And like a sheepdog I might go a big deep circuit, up through the bottom of Collins's wood, and round, fast at first and then come on stalking moccasin-light to where experience told me the bird was likeliest to be by the time I got there. I was all eyes and ears and moved as if preceding myself by the range of a gunshot or two, in the zone with my prey. It was as if I dispensed with physical presence. I have to say little escaped. By the time I was sixteen, my speed and stealth, my animal knowledge of the territory saw to that.

It would be a while before the hammered single-barrelled gun came my way, a long gun with a very tight choke. With the heavier cartridge known as a Maximum it had far greater range than most guns. My father had no equal at the very outer limits of its range, as suggested in this poem called 'Cormorant':

> I remember the day the old man shot one
> high over the house and how it folded,
> like a winded umbrella, and came down
> in a thorn bush, stone dead, neck collapsed,
> wings hooked up to dry for the last time.
> But why still, that nervous, apprehensive wonder,
> the word *skart* on my tongue for pleasure?
> Why couldn't I settle to sleep that night
> for thinking about it? I wasn't upset.
> I didn't weep. It got what was coming to it.
> It was the devil, the thief on the cross, of fish
> that we might catch. Way out of range it swerved,
> but the old man was a dead-eyed dick.
> I'd seen him perform such miracles before.
> And even if I smiled, when he laid it out
> for my education in the life and death
> of birds, and distinguished it from the *SHAG*
> I kept my school-yard smirk to myself, so he had
> no cause to curse me for a tom fool.
> Perhaps it was just those three dabs,
> the size of half-a-crown, that came
> flipping from its gullet alive, alive O
> O, O as moist as eyes? ... Maybe.

'Skart' is a Scots word for a cormorant, Gaelic 'Sgarbh' (derived I believe from Old Norse-Icelandic). Satan metamorphosed into the form of a cormorant in Eden. That's all you need to know.

The Damascus gun could not have hit the cormorant, whoever fired it. But it was legendary, and legend has always stirred me and stolen into my heart. No matter it is a dangerous thing, as Plato would surely have agreed, seeing the poetry of it, its power, in fact, to bring us down to earth. But Plato or no Plato, the gun itself bordered on the dangerous. If you cocked both its hammers at once (only one was original to the gun), firing one could trigger the other, if not reliably, unreliably, which of course in such a case is worse. Still I loved the Damascus gun above all others, even if the trigger guard all-too reliably chopped back against my second finger every time I fired and made it swell and bruised the bone, after two or three shots.

So with my gun as part of me, as quick to come to my shoulder and fire as you might blink an eye, I'd step in under the wooded hill and up into the dark wood and beyond until it was all second nature and only first nature left, the zone of intimacy, where I was, out there, beyond where I stood, with what I pursued. What I pursued might be either prey or simply the observable world in close-up and slow-motion, flora as much as fauna. For stalking imposed slow-motion on everything, and enlarged every-thing to the gaze. It was a country with extraordinary plants and flowers to find, according to their season. Shelter from the east, the drainage typical of limestone, a coastal warmth and a north-south westerly aspect, bred a rare fecundity.

Botanists have listed numerous varieties to be found on our hill and in its vicinity. I will not list them all (Pennant catalogues very many of them), but of the names I knew to identify, I remember most the dark orchids, the speedwell and the gentian. In the blackthorn and ivy-floored entangle-ment to the south of the tower great beds of violets flourished, and in a meadow beyond, at the northernmost end of Collins's wood, carpets of cowslips flowered such as I've never seen anywhere else in my life. It was a floral paradise. And a myriad bird species flitted and nested there, from the goldcrest to the tawny owl and the herring gull. And the raven lunged overhead, crossing from the Little Orme, and the cormorant winged it fast as it could back to the Little Orme, after fishing expeditions up the estuary or in the mountain lakes, or simply at sea, one eye on my father, the other far away.

The first full season we had there was autumn. For me it is always the first season, the elegiac best and worst. Worst because it heralded back-to-school. I cannot tell you the gloom that prospect gave rise to, a gloom heightened by the fact that I could see the school from the cliff, appropriately located just this side of the gasworks and the rubbish tip. Best because the birds fattened and the warmed sea in the mouth of the estuary ran with fish as at no other time of year.

It was a while yet before I awakened to the literary, in any conscious way. But by sixteen I began to find myself detained by poems, distracted by them, abstracted by them. The works of the poets began to seduce me and the lives of writers generally: authors of nature and wilderness writing above all, whether in verse or prose. I started now to save to buy books and not so much simply to feed the racing pigeons I'd begun to keep a little earlier. To which end, and to my father's disapproval, I made myself a bicycle from an old frame and bits from the tip, painted it bright yellow, and took on a paper-round. Nor was it just any round but the round of rounds: the one, there was no other, with the singular virtue of including in its compass the Welsh girl's home.

So I could go to her door every day, and deliver the *Guardian* (which had been as recently as 1959 the *Manchester Guardian*), and a little monthly magazine her father liked called *Sea Breezes*, a 'Worldwide Magazine of Ships and the Sea'. He'd served in the navy, escorting convoys, during the war. Digressions about the hardships and horrors of war endured upon the cruel sea were ever the best part of his lessons in history. In time the family would often get their papers late on Saturday morning, in the hope the Welsh girl might be up-and-about to be seen. Slip them the wrong paper and she might come out to catch you. But she never did, only her kid brother or her father himself. Sometimes if I was lucky I'd catch a glimpse of her, or hear her playing the piano. It was enough.

Then at some doomed point in my sixteenth year I started to attempt to write verse. Soon I'd be stealing home hurriedly, not always to change into my old clothes and escape with the Damascus barrelled gun, but to use my father's typewriter, laboriously to type up what I'd written, just to see it at that remove from my hand, ever an important material stage. This had to be done secretly.

Above all my father must not know. The pressure of his gaze on my words would be too much to bear. I can understand my fears. The poems were too bad. To describe them as juvenilia would be to abuse the term. Until recently I thought they'd all been destroyed, except one or two that by editorial misjudgement found publication. I binned or burned everything I could lay hands on in my late twenties, except my account of the Aran Islands.

That proved to be at the commencement of a two-decade depression, not induced by the hopeless poems but more generally at not living the dream, not writing it, with the pram in the hall and all that. But such things are all to the good in time. You must just know your mind and keep your course at heart, no matter. Either it is in you and will out or it isn't. It was a good decision and not baleful, to burn those paper bales. But some poor things from that time slipped the net. Copies survived, as have recently been brought to light by an old schoolfriend, now a retired professor, who won't relinquish what he has, except in photocopy. So I can't put them out of their misery.

Attracted at first by Keats, I began with the view that a real poem should be a poem of some length. I had little or no idea what they were about but I liked to flirt with 'Hyperion' and 'Endymion' as much as read the more accessible poems, 'To Autumn' and the odes. But I wasn't a well-wrought urn man. It was the idea of length I liked, and the promise of being able to talk.

I was ambitious. I kept two artless long poems on the boil at once, in this time of my first fumbling after the muse's favour. One was about a road across the moss to Alticry shore in Galloway (my lost sphagnum opus), the other about the Conwy estuary. Not a line of them do I have to look at now, at least not in their earliest form. They weren't remotely like Keats, either, as cannot be surprising.

A revised fragment of the estuary poem was published. It was a passage revamped when I was nineteen and approaching twenty. Conscripted into the service of a shorter poem, it appeared after some delay in the American magazine *Shenandoah*. A man called Richard Greer facilitated publication, a Fulbright scholar, and another man whose surname was Dabney. To the very best of my recollection the following from that illustrious periodical (even Homer nods) bears some resemblance to the same lines in the original, begun, I believe, when I was sixteen, and continued over a year.

> He walks out to the sea with a barbed spear
> Follows down the channel that is empty
> Looks over the horizon to the sun
> Waiting for the tide to turn back inland
> With its haul of silver and green-backed fish

Already nosing at his heart's gravel.
The sea breaks out from the slack of low tide;
Far against the sky, between the headland
And the island, the big september flood
Limps in its beginning, chokes the river
Back with salt, thrusts heads of water forward
As fast as the careful man retreats,
Slips forward, runs back from beneath itself;
The foam, mud-brown, dries down into the sand
About to vanish, is pushed on and grows
Swings deceptively in, now ankle deep
Sucks the white foot down, down the pooling land
Behind him, to more than man-deep holes.

He once saw, out beneath the point of rocks
As the tide sprang, the heavy-headed bass
Press in upon the shoaling land
Fixed to the current of the sea's hunger;
And now these fish push against him, spines bared,
Driving in the flash of the sea's teeth...

Who was that youth, writing those lines, secretly, as if
hiding them under his hand? I take some pride in him, to
think of my younger self, so intense, so fixed to his current,
so fixated, if only descriptive. Such hope heaped in him, I
wish I was in his boots today. No matter the deaths he had
to face and disappointments, until he made his way to me.
(I still have the head of his barbed spear, more properly a
tine, used for stabbing flounder, at risk of stabbing your
white foot. Also used for spearing salmon.)

I was too intense, a friend of my father once told me. No
friend of mine, I thought. But the headland and the island,
the point of rocks, those shoaling bass, how they chastened
my eye. How the sea's hunger consumed my heart. How it
all led me astray beyond reason or comprehension. How
strange it is to have been someone else, and to feel even the
slightest pulse of his purpose so many years later, like

something from another life, an earthquake's tidal after-shock.

What really increased the intensity was the copy of J.M. Synge's *The Aran Islands* I found among my father's books. The effect of this work on my mind defies rational explanation. It so touched me it couldn't have been more affecting if it had been written by the Welsh girl herself. But she was a scientist and literature didn't cause her to lift up her heart to the stars – though music did – or lead her from her path.

It would have led me from my path, if I'd been on one. Instead it became the path, the way, the road to nowhere, whether sea-road, shore road, high road or low road – I'll be on Inis Mór before you, became my philosophy. It wasn't any of Synge's twilight fairy-host stuff that took me, or the story-telling of Old Pat, reputedly founded in models from antiquity, but passages like this one:

> When we set off it was a brilliant morning of April, and the green, glittering waves seemed to toss the canoe among themselves; yet as we drew nearer this island a sudden thunderstorm broke out behind the rocks we were approaching, and lent a momentary tumult to this still vein of the Atlantic.

or this:

> The rain continues; but this evening a number of young men were in the kitchen mending nets, and the bottle of poteen was drawn from its hiding-place.
>
> One cannot think of these people drinking wine on the summit of this crumbling precipice; but their grey poteen, which brings a shock of joy to the blood, seems predestined to keep sanity in men who live forgotten in these worlds of mist.
>
> I sat in the kitchen part of the evening to feel the gaiety that was rising, and when I came into my own room after dark, one of the sons came every time the bottle made its round, to pour me out my share.

I liked the sound of Michael, Synge's guide on Inishmaan, but I wasn't hooked as Synge was by a primitivist ideal. I was more taken by those 'half-civilized fishermen', as he chose to call them, individuals he encountered on a visit to Inis Mór, the big island. These men were inclined to despise the simplicity of life on Synge's preferred middle island, Inis Meáin. They wanted to know, what still interests me: how Synge passed his time 'with no decent fishing to be looking at.'

But it was the overall Synge-song of the prose I really liked. Its rhythms soon stole my attention from itself. Strong tributary streams I found elsewhere, in late Dylan Thomas, and early, among those boys of summer in their ruin and in his estuarine 'Author's Prologue'; in the T.S. Eliot of 'Prufrock', especially the closing paragraph, and 'Dry Salvages'; in Lawrence's 'Ship of Death'; in what eventually I could understand of Baudelaire, and a very little Tristan Corbière, which I think I got at through a reference in Eliot. But you must understand these things were all seen as through a glass darkly. I was seduced symbolically. I didn't have precocious powers of understanding. I didn't need to stop to ask if I understood. The thing was different. Something in it ran away with me. I ran away with it, like a thief. I was more interested in my sensual life, which now, most passionately, included the sensual life of words.

A very little went a long way with me. So it does still. So it does here, in the same sense that often can mean rarely, and once is more than enough, as you know. A glance from the Welsh girl, for example, a dismissive glance no less than a longed-for come-hither. When I read my favourite writers I could hardly hold my eye to the page without shooting off in my own direction. I wasn't a good reader. I'm still not a good one. Nor am I a scholar any more than I am a gentleman, please my maker.

Then last of all in the genre, beyond the end of school, Richard Murphy's *Sailing to an Island* which I bought in Dublin at Green's Bookshop near Trinity College, on just turning nineteen, after a pilgrimage on my summer dreyman's Border Breweries wages, to Inis Mór, prospecting. I have the copy still, as I have most of them, above all among them: John Bright's 'Charles Jones Memorial Prize for Literature' – winner's choice: *The Plays and Poems of J.M. Synge*; but *The White Goddess*, and *Six Existentialist Thinkers...* are more recent replacements, the originals going the way of all books, as life takes one here and there. But what days they were, for that wide-eyed boy of summer in his ruin.

A longer catalogue of reading there was, but these works and authors were the most telling ones, and also fragments of MacDiarmid put my way by a Welsh nationalist autodidact, Meirion Roberts, a man who did more than anyone to broaden my reading, except perhaps the late Charles Jones, but that's a story for later, just round the corner. Meirion put Robert Graves's *Goodbye to All That* in my hand, and I loved it for the good riddance of it, the rejection of the world as ordained by one's supposed betters and the powers that be.

Your country needs you! But what ish my nation? Wales, I was born there.

Meirion would travel with my father when he came to visit me on Inis Mór to disturb my universe, to comic effect. Here's a poem that tells you more about him, and explains something of his interest in Graves's book, more concisely, 'In Memory of Private Roberts: British Soldier':

> Crossing the square in early spring,
> Wreaths withered on the memorial,
> Poppies bled by frost and snow,
> I met Private Roberts reading
> The roll call of the town's fallen.

Once

'Armistice day? My pet aversion,'
Turning to me, his lip moist,
His thorny eye narrowed like a sniper's:
'Ior Evans? He'd never spent
A night away from home before,

Buried in Mad-a-gas-car.
Corner of a foreign field?
I doubt he'd ever heard of it.
Dei Sam? on Manchester
United's books in thirty-nine:

Buried in France. I bet
He's never remembered
At the going down of the sun
Or in the morning... Duw!
You know, I often contemplate

Siegfried Sassoon, chucking his medal away.
Never applied for mine.
All the way to Tobruk without
So much as a lance-jack's stripe,
I'm proud to say.

And Francis Ledwidge, born
The same day as Hedd Wyn,
And killed, you know, the same day
And in the same place too.
His comment: "To be called

A British soldier
While my country has
No place among nations..."
He'd marched to Vesuvius
With Marcus Aurelius

In one breast-pocket and
The *Mabinogi* in the other,
An old campaigner
Over bog and heather
To find and fish the Serw stream:

Elusive, stubborn thread of water,
Of stygian glooms and mountain glances,
Its limpid, garrulous medium,
'Full,' as he said, 'of small trout
The length of a youth's hand.'

Meirion also lent me in their slender and deeply moving
first editions *The Stones of the Field*, first published by the
Druid Press in Carmarthen in the year of my birth, and *An
Acre of Land*, printed in Newtown, Montgomery, in 1952,
by R.S. Thomas. There was hardly anything Meirion hadn't
read, from a slender essay by Virginia Woolf about going to
purchase a pencil, to Gibbon's *Decline and Fall*, to Logan
Pearsall Smith's *Trivia*, from the work of Mary Webb (O
Precious Bane!) to that of Alun Lewis and *In Parenthesis* by
David Jones. He was an inspiration, his gates wide open to
the written word and his insight into the colonial situation
light-years ahead of the view elsewhere. For sheer intelli-
gence, humour, passion and rootedness he had no equal.
He was a postcolonialist *avant-la-lettre* and so was I under
his influence, whether I knew it or not; and I certainly knew
it if not in name when I entered the unknown world. It was
a revelation, and one that has never waned.

It was the sea and the literature of the sea I loved most.
I remember particularly being stirred by Joshua Slocum's
marvellous sea-going story: *Sailing Alone Around the World*.
But it's not so much that I was so taken by the writings I
refer to, which in the wider world is something unremark-
able, but that as to Aran I held to my resolve. More than
once or twice I'd tell my parents, at sixteen and seventeen
and more, that one day I was going to live on Inis Mór. How
was this? It seemed so unlikely a thing they merely smiled,
in the spirit of 'one day you'll grow up' my son. How
pleased I am now to know how wrong they were, especially
about the growing up. The way to grow is circular, longest

way round, shortest home. Up is a big mistake. Down into mind and round is best.

Who says poetry makes nothing happen, Synge being all poetry, verse or prose? There is no circumstance in which nothing happens. But the assertion burdens poetry with irrelevant expectation. There's the strongest case for saying it makes everything happen, that it's prior to all other verbal forms of expression, vision, and thought. The poets precede the theologians and philosophers and stand elsewhere from them, looking awry. Here's my poem of it. I call it 'Synge-Song':

> I was one after your own heart
> or so I thought, neither landed
> nor gentry, but blew ashore
> aboard your limpid pages,
> to Inis Mór and there I stranded.
> My mind blown away
> and all at sea for nevermore.
>
> The curragh also wears a thin partition.
> I've felt the sea-pulse beneath it
> through my hand, life itself,
> inside out, outermost to be
> inmost in the world.
> Get out more, you who say
> poetry makes nothing happen.
>
> Be-in-the world and see:
> the poem is earthbound
> and elsewhere to the day
> as any playboy knows
> down the passage of recorded time
> through calm and storm
> the first to make landfall.

There is or there was once a strong case for saying all mental landscapes in the western world would be profoundly different if Wordsworth hadn't written his *Lyrical Ballads* and its preface, or 'The Prelude', which also overtook my life at this time, no less than is clearly true in the case of Homer's *Odyssey*, no matter nothing happens without hearer or reader. One or two of either at critical historical moments are enough to bend the world's bias and change the horizons of humankind.

Just a small work of words can set the world atilt. Forget your global network. When the power goes down in the post-apocalypse, and the visionaries rise from the rubble what use your password and your headlong hurry, you intelpentium? Where is your digitized archive now? You need no password to encounter a poem, spoken or read, oral or written, to nourish your soul before whoever your maker is. Remember that as you scavenge among the ruins of Rome? But those scavengers won't be of your kind. They'll be the descendants of those who scavenge now. Of whom there is no shortage and never has been down the course of time.

To be sure, a little can go such a long way it can reach to the crack of doom, like the Anglo-Saxon poem 'The Wanderer'.

★ ★ ★

Or the 'Sea-farer'.... An element to account for here, beyond the shore, is the sea itself. The sea plays with horizon more thoroughly than anything on earth, than night and day together. I first took to its magical perspectives in yet another ritual connected with my passing the eleven plus. Not only did that singular occasion entail the Black Lake, as you know. It also saw an unprecedented act of extravagance and expenditure by my grandpa. He was otherwise, you know already, rightly deemed the very epitome of a penny-pinching Scotsman. But my little success so pleased him he stunned the known world and took me out for the day, aboard the *St Tudno*, from Llandudno pier, a steamer as they say, though there was no steam involved, to Menai Bridge on Anglesey.

Forget that we played bowls there or before coming home stopped at the fun-fair and rode the dodgems by the gates to Llandudno pier – all staggering indulgences, never witnessed before or again in grandpa's company.

The important thing for me is that I made my foundational sea-voyage then, my maiden voyage. I had been out off Ynys Enlli in a little mackerel-fishing boat. I'd whizzed a circuit of the inlet at Traeth Coch, powered by a Seagull, as you know. I had a taste for it. But this was a voyage, such as on a more dramatic scale the *Naomh Eanna* made to Kilronan pier and the islands, as later I would love. And it whetted my appetite and fuelled my longing. I've never forgotten it, even if we never lost sight of land. (That would come, on trips to the Isle of Man, as also sailed from Llandudno for a time.)

Often is one thing, once another. I saw the Orme swing round and shrink in our wake. I saw the Creuddyn sink in sea-haze, islanding the Orme, as fascinated and delighted me. I saw the seabirds – the razorbills, and puffins too, the different gulls, the cormorants – whizz in and out from the headland cliffs. I heard and saw the sea run and break, and felt the sure foot of the vessel slide and gather. I breathed the hot air of the engine room, mingled with the salty ozone of the sea. I saw Penmaenmawr, and Puffin Island close up, crowded with seabirds, and the lighthouse, and heard the clang of the bell at Penmon. I saw the pretty doll's house frontage of Beaumaris. I saw Snowdonia on the other shore roll and shift, rearranging its ranges, as we went by. I experienced the strange dream-element that is the world at sea, on a halcyon day. I saw the straits narrow and its currents race on Menai's shore. It whetted my appetite and more. I went under like a cormorant that'd not surface again until it reached Galway Bay, however many years away, in November 1968. My life over again. So breath-taking was it and heart-stopping, it drowned me for good and ill.

The *St Tudno* was my maiden voyage, innocent and virgin. The few trips that would follow later, putting out from Conwy on the fishmonger Mr Arundale's trawler were last nails in Queequeg's coffin for me. Call me Ishmael. They still haunt me, above all biding the tide after nightfall, to enter the river and come home to harbour. The *What-Ho!* was a decked lugger of a once-popular local design. I doubt she was much more than a forty-footer. She had a mast and a short brown sail. Above all she was powered by an Ailsa Craig, over-powered it might be said, but all to the good, by a big engine.

The name 'Ailsa Craig' meant a lot to me, the mysterious, burdened way names can mean to us. I had seen the Ailsa Craig, also known as 'Paddy's Milestone', with the naked eye of childhood, the granite dome off the Ayrshire coast, from which the engine took its name. This pleased me and merged the two in my mind. It made me remember the harbour at Girvan, with its trawler fleet of those days.

Curling stones are traditionally made of Ailsa Craig granite. I have two for heirlooms on my doorstep at home. My Wigtownshire farming relations and their like used to put such stones on the gateposts to their retirement bungalows. So the name 'Ailsa Craig' weighs for me resonantly, the full weight of its granite. What's in a name? Worlds of meaning, 'Ailsa Craig':

> I voyaged with you once
> beating like my heart
> right through me,
> whatever the opposite is

to weak knees, weakness,
a balancing act, and now
I anchor in memory
on those wild seas.

I cannot ground but fathom
where I am, sitting on
a doorstep, here at home,
running a hand over
a granite curling stone,
an heirloom and horizon
sixty million years ago,
I remember seeing you.

Mr Arundale had been a commander in the Navy during the war. He loved the sea and knew it like the back of his hand, saw into it with his grey eyes, and read the weather as if he knew it by heart. He had just that much of Ahab about him to keep you guessing. I suppose he was a hobby fisherman, but it was a hobby that served his shop with the freshest fish on the coast.

So it came that I shipped aboard the *What-Ho!* under Mr Arundale, first with my father and then, far better, on my own. I remember being early and killing time on the quay, haunting there, relishing the expectancy in the morning air, as the tide rose in the river and the river rose in the tide, and the vessels beat a foot to the gathering rhythm and kicked their keels to be off. I felt myself into it, into the role of the sea-going fisherman, deckhand trawlerman. Compared with the all-weather real thing aboard the boats that would go away for several days, it was like poaching in Collins's Wood: all the kicks without the risks. But drowning is drowning. Just as you might say never trust a horse, never trust the sea.

Nor was there anything half-hearted about it when Mr Arundale arrived amid the bustle of fishermen and mid-morning idlers and holidaying lookers-on. He took command. You had to look lively and haul in the pram and lower the supplies and lower yourself. The pram only took two, oarsman and crew of one at a time. It sat deep in the tide at that, quick to turn on an oar, like a gull on its webbed foot turning smartly to feed on something passing swiftly by in the stream, the flood from the mountains. There across the way where the river ran hidden the *What-Ho!* rode at her mooring, all ship-shape. She looked somehow businesslike, as if a vessel might put on its experience and purpose and wear them with vigour, restless as a thoroughbred for the tide-race, throwing her head up against her mooring.

So then you got aboard her and looked back across the waters at the floating harbour and riding castle town. Who'd ever want to live ashore again? Who'd want to come back to the humdrum world of the dull lubber, the hidebound burgher? Except that coming and going, putting out and making landfall, are heart and soul of it. In which spirit I commend to you the fare forward of it, and fare well but not farewell, as the Ailsa Craig starts up with a great throb, like a heart throb, and the waters rouse with a deep churning as she gets the bit between her teeth. Is this the death-wish under us as the stern bites in and takes a step down, to bring the prow up, or so it feels, like an orgasm, an acceleration, a surge? I always think so. And so too at this moment, as away we went, it felt not so much as if we were bound to our fishing ahead, as rushing from our haven astern.

Down the channel we ran between the now submerged shellfish banks, out by Morfa, and round beyond Penmaen-bach to shoot our net down the Fairway, down to the Lavan Sands, beyond Penmaenmawr. There are few things more intoxicating, in all the fishings I've undertaken, than being slewed there between trawl and tide butting down that sea-road, like driving with the brakes on, as the otter boards resist the flow and keep the wings of the net wide. From where you are, the sea runs round the world, and you feel part of its immensity, suspended in time, until it's time to haul and gravity returns for a while, against the backdrop of the floating world.

We'd have a couple of shots down that way, the bulging sock of the net when we swung it up, spilling plaice, flounder and thornback skate, barnacled crabs and cobbles, shocks of glistening weed, a bather's plimsoll but happily no bather, and so on. Then we'd run out round Puffin Island, trolling for mackerel, with hand-lines, four and six at a time, and if we hit them, pause to wallow and hit them hard, feathering vertically, so the boxes rattled and splattered with them as they filled, before we shot again by Table Road, out off Traeth Coch.

It seemed we had all the time in the world there, shoaled together. But the tide waits for no man, and with one last haul on board, we'd beat for home, the Ailsa Craig drumming hard, vibrating under us, the *What-Ho!* with the bit between her teeth, galloping, and night rising up and the stars shoaling so near you'd think you might shoot your net at them, in the topsy-turvy seaborne world. Now we've been too quick for it and must hove-to, to nose forward little by little. Mussels crunch under us. At the water's edge, all round, oyster-catchers and sandpipers make their music, pipe their chorus to the stars, as the dark engulfing tide chivvies them. Up they wheel into the chill night air, piping and whistling, to re-alight and fish for their supper and sing for it, again. Over and over they retreat with the water, heard but not seen, unless as a faint glimmer or aura, until the tide is in, and silence seems to fill the world, for a moment if no more.

So it was. There in the midst of it, the Ailsa Craig chugged and spluttered and sang to us, and the *What-Ho!*

told us the story of her life, in every creak and dark recess of her, wooed to it by the river at her shoulders, the sea at her stern. We had our catch all gutted and sung for, except not all the thornback skate were skinned. So we worked on at them, feeling the cold now, hands cut and raw, the very dream itself, except for the one behind it.

I'd up and walk from my wage-slavery tomorrow to do that again. Though there's no again only another time. Once it would be, in itself, however freighted with past remembrance. But no one invites me. Mr Arundale is long-gone under the sea. I know no one with a boat. I'm a mere harbourer of thoughts and memories. All I do I do in mind, then set out in pen and ink, a fisher of tropes and expression. Make fast. This is the last fishing ground, as yet not known to any other. Shoot your sentence here, I urge myself at break of day this morning. Run out your spillet and trammel, your seines of sense, trawl-tales as tall as the sea at the mind's stormy rim. Be buoyant in spite of all. Why? To show courage in ignoring death. Pour encourager les autres. Fare forward. Plough on. Having put your hand to the wheel, don't look back. Even at the cry 'Man overboard!' hold to your course, go overboard with a passion. Haul in your catch. Live with your luck. Make your luck. Be a Makar. Don't look back.

But it's all looking back and longing too.

Just so I'd look back after the Welsh girl when we passed. Look back I did and long, even for simple acknowledgement. But she showed no interest, no matter I studied hard to cross her path, to gaze on her, her pale cheek, her raven hair, her attitude so composed and quietly purposeful. I didn't exist for her, which only heightened her allure. The fateful afternoon was now not far away when I'd wait at the far school gate by the canteen to ask her, stepping forward from the wall, to speak to her for the first time. No one ever waited there for any other purpose. Though it wasn't the first time I'd waited. Just the first time my courage held and she wasn't with her friends, two other medics in the making. How absurd my aspiration! But such is or was the onus on the male to propose and the female to dispose. She took no time disposing of me.

'I'm going out with Max,' she said without pause or blush and stepped back on her way. It was a blow, as you can guess. Yet, incorrigible, I found comfort in the moment as well as disappointment. She could have shown outright scorn but she didn't. She'd spoken to me at least, and I to her. There was no put-down but the knock-back made me deliver papers much earlier for a few weeks, so as not to run the risk of meeting her. But nothing changed. I did not move on. And now, little by little my passion grew beyond obsession into the wilder realms of idealisation. It was as if I lived a script by Petrarch or by Dante, though I'm sure I'd never heard of either. My day would come.

Or night, anyway, the night of the school dance. They'd given lessons in the Gay Gordons and the like, the waltz, over several evenings before the night itself. I was no dancer. Nor was she among the girls with whom we tried to learn our steps. But I went to all the lessons. No rock-and-roll here.

I remember my mother scoring the soles of my new black shoes with a kitchen fork to give them grip. I remember plunging off down the black lane, skidding about, turning my ankle, in those inappropriate, pinching shoes, and walking the three miles to school, in a suit and tie. The hall lights shone out and for perhaps the only time in my life I went to school with a light and eager step. Did I know something? I did not. I didn't even know if she'd be there. I merely hoped against hope. But there she was, in a white dress with blue polka dots, and her hair newly cut the way she wore it, short, so the hairline ran just below the jawline, and parted in the middle so she seemed to look at you with her big hazel eyes from between two black curtains, each ending in a little sweep, upwards. I can see her now, and those bottle-green suede high heels she turned on as she danced.

It should be said that by this time, while I kept as ever my two worlds, moving between the scholars and the wilder boys, with the strongest friendships in both camps, I'd drawn attention to myself. I was the literary one. Now and then I'd taken one or other of the more priggish masters by surprise with my eccentric reading. As with the one I thought a stuffy one who eventually deserted for an English public school in the South Downs where clearly he'd be more at home. What he said – it was about Maupassant – I don't remember. Something perhaps about realism and peasant life. He was the junior French master. He alluded to W.H. Hudson. He was sure we'd never heard of W.H. Hudson, a wonderful writer. But indeed I had read *A Shepherd's Life*, the very book he had in mind, as I could tell. I knew a good deal about W.H. Hudson. My father revered and loved him. I can still see the surprise on the master's face. Reasonably enough, he'd always thought we were every last one of us as ignorant as the day we were born.

W.H. Hudson and Richard Jefferies had been for a spell my staple reading, though Synge was my master, the orchestrator of the dream. So pleased to realise all this was the poet manqué Leonard Brookes, my English teacher, long since not of this world, that he gave me his own copy of Edward Thomas's life of Jefferies, the first thing by Thomas I ever read. I was blessed in all this and advantaged in coming from the home I did. I had a head's start, for once. It no longer mattered that I was an innumerate daydreamer. Though I was no scholar, as you know.

Though I wasn't really a reader but one for the kickstart tasting, as still I am. I was none the less no longer entirely beyond the pale.

So at one point or another in the latter part of the evening, I caught the Welsh girl's eye between dances, and in that look saw what I'd lived and died a thousand deaths for: a come hither, a louch look as they say in Scots. I danced with her. Nor would I be backward in coming forward. I monopolised her, we monopolised each other and danced the three last dances together, and the last smooch more intimately than any of the others dared. Nods and smiles and jokes there were among the supervising teachers. It was as if we'd gone just a step to the very edge of going too far. But would she let me walk her home? She would if she could but she couldn't. Her father etc etc.... So I walked home alone, or flew. For I was in outer space, and my thoughts went flying everywhere.

But where did this leave me when I came back to earth?

I don't know where it left me. But it found me the next night after a day's euphoria braving the doorbell to my fate. My body took me to her door, as if in slow-motion, as if dragging the Earth behind it.

'I knew it was you,' she said with quiet passion, 'I knew', in a hurried whisper. How with the foresight of hindsight we know these things when we're in love.

'Will you come out with me?'

What did I think, after that dancing...? She was just delivering the bad news to Max or Brad or whoever (the class of their names spoke volumes), back from the university for Christmas, and ever hopeful. *Yes... yes... yes...* she would. She would. I wanted to kiss her at once but could give no indication, I was so overcome. I still can't believe my lucky stars. I certainly couldn't believe them then. Disbelief threw me back into orbit, to go and look a little closer at those stars, to believe my eyes, into the wildest orbit I can remember, bar one (euphoria at the Black Lake, in the estuary, or on Inis Mór being of a different, steadier order).

It was a cold December night. The stars were up above the wooded hill. And the hill held dark chasms where the trees stood, dark as any allegorical dark wood ever portrayed in life's way. The sea ran on the coast, just audibly. And the town went about its business, oblivious that a miracle had taken place while I walked and then ran through the streets up to Tan-y-Bryn Road and, instead of plunging up our rocky road, ran on round to Nant-y-Gammar hill. Yuri Gagarin never made a bigger or faster orbit of the known world than my lap of honour that night.

Nant-y-Gammar is a narrow hill road of steep gradient. But I ran, the loneliness of the long-distance runner my forte at that time. No gravity could hold me back. On I ran, talking to myself, urging myself on, calling her name, my name, in wild exclamation. *Yes! Yes!* I shouted to the night. Talk about possession. Whoever said it is only nine-tenths of the law never set eyes on the Welsh girl. I got onto the heath, way back beyond our property. The surge of energy released in me by her *yes, yes...* was surely as manic then as it is comic to consider now. I ran on, climbed the high estate wall and jumped down into the conifer planting. The trees there being not yet established, the planting was entangled and overgrown underfoot. But I leapt and bolted through it on to the ancient deciduous woods of Gloddaeth.

Pheasants spurted up about me from the planting like fireworks as I went. I took no care whether Mr Groom the gamekeeper might be about or not. Pegasus couldn't have caught me as I raced on down the hill now, through the great shadowy wood, deciduous and bare, except for loomings of yew and cedar that suddenly obscured the stars. Believe them? They filled my head. Then I broke on down through a little run of hazel and saplings until I met the low wall, at the back of the big house.

A peacock trailing stars behind it flew in wild terror from its roost on the high wall, at my sudden descent, and laboured with a peacock cry, to settle in a tree above me. Such a din! I ran a little faster now, for the path was a dark and shadowy trap, until I got beyond it, beyond the lodge house in the corner of the field, where a dog had begun to bark. I ran out to the foot of the bryn, and on, accelerating as if for the finishing line at Marathon, till I reached home, my heart still hardly quiet, in the wake of her acceptance.

So it was my life entered a fourth dimension.

Now instead of stealing glances into the front-room as I delivered the *Guardian*, I could sit in it, while my beloved played the piano, or did her homework, so that we could go out. I could talk with her there, in the chaos of that room which accommodated in pillars the dispersed library of the late Charles Jones, B. Litt. (whose memorial prize I'd won). Here I found undreamt of treasures. It became my own private library. All the poets in library editions were there and many another thing that shaped my reading as not even the combination of my father and Meirion Roberts could have done. There were books and there was a gramophone too. Now we'd sit entwined on the sofa together listening to works by Beethoven, Rachmaninov, Grieg, Sibelius, Dvorák, Smettana, Tchaikovsky.

For me it was the first time I heard such works. I applied myself to them. I applied myself to her. I realise now that the preference in that household for such a high proportion of nationalist music was an expression of Welsh passion by other means. Not that the great Welsh choral performances were silent there. Not that the family was as Welsh as it might have been. There was Liverpool-Welsh in them, and a strain from Manchester. The Welsh girl's mother was a fay

one though, and her mother seemed to me as Welsh as they
come, a one-eyed, glass-eyed granny, sea-widow, living on
Menai Strait at Waterloo. There sometimes the Welsh girl
went into purdah to study and I'd be allowed down for an
afternoon, perhaps to see her.

High culture and Welsh culture notwithstanding, 'Top of
the Pops', in the era of 'The Supremes' and 'Ike and Tina
Turner' (river deep, mountain high), didn't go neglected by
the Welsh girl either, all that stuff about love-me-do and not
being able to get enough satisfaction. Here was sexuality
manifest, just as our own was compelling us towards each
other in our all-embracing dream of each other.

By comparison up under the wooded hill we were hardly
a musical household. We had only recently acquired a
record-player. My sister, away to train as a speech-thera-
pist, encountered jazz in England, at concerts promoted by
Norman Granz. It was the era of Acker Bilk too, whose
'Stranger on the Shore' I taught myself to play on an old
clarinet, with n'er a lesson. But I soon departed from that
and moved on from my sister's taste too, for the like of John
Lewis and the MJQ. Less prim African-American music
became my obsession, a music of the body and the soul,
speaking to the wrongs not just of history but of America
there and then, with proud and brilliant virtuosity.

Jazz was hard to come by in North Wales. Everything
was hard to come by. I once set out to hitch-hike from
Llandudno to Bangor to go to a specialist French-language
bookshop there, in pursuit of work by nineteenth-century
poets. It was a little shop near the university. No one would
stop for me, so I ended up walking all the foot-weary way
there, eighteen miles, only to find the shop had just closed.
But I did come by jazz records: Thelonius Monk my first,
most intense, personal discovery; Lester Young, Lucky
Thompson, Johnny Griffin, Dexter Gordon, Roland Kirk,

John Coltrane – all the horn men....

But here by the guiding light of the Welsh girl my horizons shifted and looked up even more, and my life changed. She even arranged for us to go to hear the Welsh National Opera perform 'Madam Butterfly' at the Odeon. I didn't take to it. Little could I have guessed then that decades later I'd go with a friend to a brilliant performance of that most tragic and painful work, in Los Angeles. High up in the gods there, and blasted almost senseless by jetlag as I was, it still swept me up, and roused me too, vividly to recall my first night at the opera, in the kissing seats at the back of the Odeon, with my first love.

But all that excitement of discovery was as nothing against the intoxication of her presence walking with me, down Clarence Road to go to the pictures, for the first time, hand in hand, like Adam and Eve entering the unknown world together, as if forever. I can still hear those bottle-green suede shoes with the high heels clack and click as she stepped along chattering and laughing. I can still see the skirt of her light fawn tweedy coat swing from her waist as she strode and its suede collar and pocket flaps. I can still see her paleness highlighted by her raven-black hair. I can still feel her hand in mine, fingers interlocked, as in a dream. So it was.

I would know such intoxication again. But twice is impossible. And once is always enough.

A man's life no more than to say not just one, as Hamlet said, but once.... Then nevermore.

THE UNKNOWN WORLD

What world lay beyond Wales? What tempting but uneasy world beyond the moors and mountains, over the hills and far away, down-river of the Dee, beyond the marches, on Severn side, the promiscuous border counties, where dwell the Welnglish and Engelsh, and Wenlock Edge, and Housman's poems that by now I'd learnt to love?

At eighteen I could count on the fingers of one hand the number of occasions on which I'd spent spells of time in England. (I don't count here the night-drives that brought us at dawn to Gretna Green and Dumfries and led to idyllic holidays in Galloway, tearful to leave: night drives as if to protect our delicate souls from England in the light of day.)

It wasn't that I didn't want to escape. I was restive to be gone, to leave my father's house and be my own man, or whatever I might become. But for all its certainties, the soul of life in youth is all ambivalence, wavering unquiet, and Prince of Denmark indecision. The world beyond Wales I would enter, in my first clear step from home to independence, would be the dark Satanic North of England. I went with hope to study the philosophers and poets, but above all to join the Welsh girl there. But I dwelt unhappily in the great throng of the world, the unknown world, too well-known by my more knowing peers for a backwoods backward Black Lake boy like me to survive in.

It is no sin to lose your way, though you might be excused for thinking it so. I soon lost my way anyway and abandoned all pretence at study. I read only what I wanted to read and attended lectures sporadically if I did. Not that I knew what I was doing. It seems like immodesty perhaps but I think it was far more modest than that. It was misery and depression. I was grieving, that's what I was doing. I followed two courses loyally and closely: Geoffrey Hill on 'Poetry from Yeats to Hughes and Gunn', and Quentin Bell on aesthetics, 'bad art', and Victorian painting. Otherwise I played truant. I found bits of urban wilderness to mooch in and wrote poems. I found old city pubs to drink in and be melancholy. I wasn't homesick. I was out of my element, like the albatross on the pavement. Once in a way I was summoned to appear before a Dean, a man called Smith. I'm sure he was a decent person and only doing his job, but to me he was an officious policeman and I detested him. The truth is I was depressed and miserable in my circumstances. It is a common story. I was resisting the call to grow up. And that wasn't entirely unvirtuous, the way 'up' was defined. Or I had to meet my Moral Tutor, a philosopher called Cameron, a quiet thoughtful and feeling man he seemed who interpreted 'Moral' and 'Tutor' in a very liberal way, making it clear, if not saying as much explicitly, that I must take responsibility for my own actions, or indeed as in this context was meant, inactions.

Christmas summoned me home early, to see my father in hospital, after he'd narrowly escaped death in a road accident. It proved a fateful time of regression, haunting again the cliffs and woods, shooting Lord Mostyn's pheasants where I could, or putting up a woodcock from the frosty leaf-bed, mooching at the borders of the day, or down on the estuary as the tides ran, checking nightlines, digging bait to set them again, in the cold salt air, in hope of plaice or flounder or stray codling. And the weather ran in spate about the Wooded Hill, roaring in the harried pines, as if the world was all at sea, and not just young Andrew McNeillie, Mac an Filidh (son of the poet or poets).

It was then that the whole starry-eyed beauty of that coast, the long sea-race roar, the rush of river, the jackdaws blown over the bryn, the wheeling seabirds above the rubbish tip, spilling over the bay, haloing the Norseman's Orme's head, wavering in the wake of Conwy trawlers; and the magic triangle of the Red Wood, the Black Lake, the

Wooded Hill, the mountains beyond, and the straits, the islands, headlands, harbours, jetties and piers, reinforced itself in me, and I read my poets, and I read my prose, my Synge and Thoreau, my *Six Existentialist Thinkers* and wrote my poems of no promise that shortly began to appear in the *Anglo-Welsh Review* and I speculated on Inis Mór, where just that previous summer my summer wages had taken me to reconnoitre. I wrote. I scribbled long poems and short poems, to little avail, but my own interest in the struggle.

Meanwhile the other kind of writing was in the making: the writing on the wall of my fate. And down I fell as it foretold. And back I came again to Wales, but very soon away from home, where I was unwelcome, my parents having little or no sympathy for me, in my failure. Call me Ishmael. (And he shall be a wild man...) So I went South, an outcast, to Rhydamman, an anthracite mining village then, where for a fiver-a-week and penny-a-line, I began the reporting and journalistic career that would take me next briefly to Liverpool, then to Broadcasting House, to sit opposite the young John Simpson, to write stories from reports filed by the likes of John Humphreys. They were the days when Alvar Liddell still read the news, in his extraordinarily sonorous voice. (I once half fell in love with his daughter at a party.) Almost my last triumph – and I had one or two in that line – was a nailbiting last-minute minute-and-a-half's-worth for Saturday's foreshortened 'World at One' bulletin. It was a story from the TUC's last day at Blackpool, General Secretary George 'Eyebrows' Woodcock the man of the hour, and John Humphreys the correspondent whose copy I condensed, even as it still came spilling from the machine, thinking on the spot, standing to dictate my story to my allocated typist, sitting beside me. And next... hell-for-leather and adrenalin rush down to the studio, almost as in steam-radio days, in the nick of time.

Then very shortly afterwards, at the tender age of twenty-two, I resigned before a Board about to promote me to be a Senior ...what I don't remember, to leave for Inis Mór, rather in the spirit of Auden's line, 'Leave for Cape Wrath to-night'.

I left by night train from Euston with all my worldly goods to catch the Liverpool ferry for Dublin. I had wrath in me too at the way of the world and the poetry of departure coursed in my youthful veins as the salt-sea coursed round the world. And the rest of this story I have told already.

The Author

Andrew McNeillie is a Professor of English at the University of Exeter. He was born in 1946, in Hen Golwyn, in North Wales, and educated at the John Bright Grammar School, Llandudno, and Magdalen College, Oxford. He was until recently Literature Editor at Oxford University Press.

His new book is the belated prequel to an acclaimed memoir *An Aran Keening* (Lilliput Press, 2002), an account of his stay for just short of a year on Inis Mór, in 1968-69, one of the three Aran Islands at the mouth of Galway Bay. He is the founder of the Clutag Press and of the literary magazine *Archipelago*, which provides the focus of a new MA at Exeter University's Cornish campus: Nature, Writing and Place.

His new poetry collection *In Mortal Memory* will appear in February 2010. He has published three volumes of poetry: *Nevermore* (2000), shortlisted for the Forward Prize best first collection; *Now, Then* (2002) and *Slower* (2006), all from Carcanet. His biography of his father the Scottish rural novelist and nature writer: *Ian Niall: Part of his Life* was published in 2007. He is a member of Academi Gymreig.